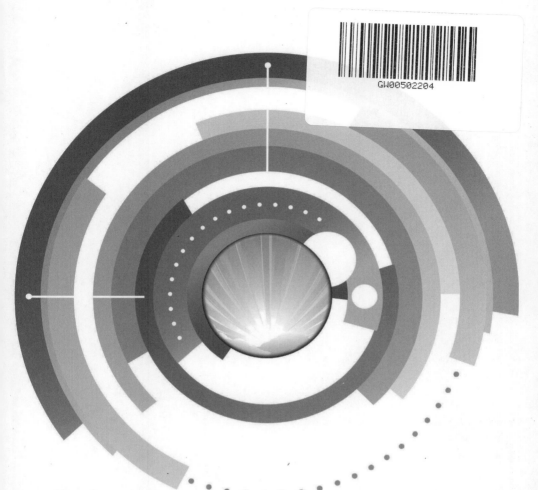

The Client-centred Financial Adviser

The ultimate guide to
building high-trust,
high-profit relationships
and a thriving practice

John Dashfield

The Client-centred Financial Adviser © John Dashfield

ISBN 978-1-909116-24-5

eISBN 978-1-909116-25-2

Published in 2015 by SRA Books

Printed in the UK by TJ International, Padstow.

Testimonials

'John has created the most cutting edge book available for financial planners today. The book reveals how today's financial planner can develop the client-centred thinking that leads to creating an exceptional client experience, which is the foundation of a prosperous and growing financial planning practice.

'This book will add more meaning and purpose to your work as a financial planner because it goes beyond techniques and gets right to the very core of how to unlock more of your potential.'

Philip Piggins, Wealth Management Partner at True Potential Wealth Management and Education Officer for the Surrey Region of the Personal Finance Society

'*The Client-centred Financial Adviser* is a book that encourages financial planners to enter a deeper level of relationship with clients. As a practising financial planner, I have been guilty of staying on the surface of a relationship, perhaps fearful of moving out of my comfort zone when engaging with clients.

'What this excellent book has highlighted to me is the massive potential that is missed when building client relationships and how these relationships could be so much better. There are also numerous practical tips and examples to help translate the theory in to reality, something that much of the material in this area does not provide.

'John Dashfield also has an excellent writing style which is easy on the eye and easy to absorb. If you are a financial planner who really wants to engage more deeply with clients, this is for you, I highly recommend it.'

Marco Vallone, Brighton Financial Ltd

'Clarity is the word that defines the experience of reading John's book.

'Following the instructions on how best to read his book, I absorbed the information the first time around, rather than analyse it. In doing so, the simplicity of his position on the client-centred experience that should be at the heart of a successful adviser's practice, was amazingly cogent.

'This was ably assisted by the style – easily read headings, well set out points and the most incredible contributions by practitioners.

'I was simply blown away by the experience of reading it and can't wait to go back for a second and third helping to follow the tenets of his arguments and add more depth and structure to my own working methods and philosophy.'

Jeannie Hainsworth Lamb, Managing Director, Lighthouse Connections (UK) Limited

'John has the ability to make you reset your thinking so that you can approach a meeting, task or problem with a clear mind. This has allowed me to really engage in free thinking financial planning with my clients where I can hear what they are saying and they know they are being heard.'

John Rook is a Certified Financial Planning practitioner and a Director and owner of Kench & Co Financial Services Ltd

'If you've been frustrated by your inability to make the progress you want, or spent ages trying to incorporate other people's ideas into your business and been left more confused than ever this book is truly eye-opening. Just switch off your logical brain and take on board the principles provided to understand how to really make a difference in your clients' lives and your own.'

Ian Kemp, CERTIFIED FINANCIAL PLANNER^{CM} professional, D J Lawrence & Associates

'Without being overly technical, John explores many of the issues that advisers face when dealing with people and what advisers can do to improve their behaviours and thus the client experience. Subjects such as how to delve deeper into client conversations, how to help clients to create meaningful goals and how to help clients to solve their own problems are covered in a comprehensive and pragmatic way. John clearly understands that to be fully engaged with and really help our clients, to the point where financial advice is a positive life-changing experience, advisers need to drop the traditional financial adviser agenda of trying to sell product, and move into the coaching space where they are uniquely positioned to bring the money and the meaning together.

'If you are an adviser who wishes to change his or her own behaviours in order to really improve client outcomes this book is a must read, it will help you to talk less, listen more and in so doing have much more powerful conversations.'

Dominic Spalding, Expert Wealth Management, Chartered Financial Planners and Independent Financial Advisers

'An invaluable insight into the psychology, emotions and cognitions of both financial planners and their clients, including well-defined suggestions on how to optimise business relationships and client experiences. Essential reading for the open-minded planner.'

Miles Hesketh MSc Marketing (Dist), Marketing Manager, Prestwood Software Ltd

'John's book is a gift of years of his experience to deliver real value in helping financial advisers achieve their potential and perform at their highest level. This thought provoking book perfectly explains and reinforces the importance of "state of mind", how people can learn to understand the concept, and then practically apply it for success, I believe, both in and outside the workplace.

'Psychological functioning is the biggest factor in performance, and coupled with a business that is completely client centric, John will help you move up different levels in profitably serving people.'

Lee Travis, CEO New Model Business Academy

'John's book articulates, in a highly accessible way, what is right at the heart of being a "client-centred" adviser. He takes you beyond techniques and into a deeper understanding of why our way of being is the most important factor in creating high trust relationships. If you want to make a bigger impact with your clients then absorb what this book reveals to you and enjoy the results.'

Simon Booth, Managing Director, Chartered Financial Planner, Foresight Independent Financial Planning

'John's book, *The Client-centred Financial Adviser* is a "manual for life, not just business!"

'Before I met John I had been an independent financial adviser for twenty years, doing the same thing, looking after the same group of clients and pretty much stuck in my ways. I had become stale, needy and under pressure from the daily battle to sign, sign, sign. Through John's coaching and what he is sharing in his book I discovered that my thinking controlled everything.

'I found that by serving my clients, truly listening with a more open and relaxed mind, by genuinely wanting to help not to sell, lead to much more insightful conversations and stronger, more enjoyable relationships. As a consequence, my business has flourished.

'John's mantra of "needy is creepy" is so true. Why as advisers do we put ourselves through the embarrassment of trying too hard to make things happen? Why are we so attached to an outcome? Why chase the signature of someone we don't really have a mutual relationship with or even particularly like? It's futile, demoralising and actually stops us dealing with the people we actually enjoy working with.

'John shares a life-changing understanding in a way that is engaging, thought provoking and makes ultimate sense. It challenges our conventional wisdom, which is why I highly recommend reading this book.'

Geoff Buckland, Chartered Financial Planner

Acknowledgments

Writing this book turned out to be a far bigger project than I, at first, imagined. I had some ideas I wanted to share, began to write and then realised it was going to be far more than a one-man job. I also realised just how many people have contributed to teaching, coaching, mentoring, supporting and encouraging me along the way.

My sincere and heartfelt thanks and appreciation goes to:

Katri, Tom and Katie for your unconditional love and support.

Michael Neill for introducing me to the inside-out paradigm.

My fellow Super Coaches for their friendship, wisdom and inspiration.

All the wonderful coaches, teachers and mentors I've learned from along the way: Annika Hurwitt, Fiona Jacob, George and Linda Pransky, Aaron Turner, Mara Gleason, Dicken Bettinger, Rudi and Jenny Kennard, Elsie Spittle, Keith Blevens, Barb Patterson, Craig Polsfuss, Dave Rogers and Christina Hall.

To Sydney Banks whose extraordinary insights are truly making our world a better place.

Sue Richardson, Liz Gooster and the team at Sue Richardson Associates for turning a rough manuscript into a finished book.

My clients for showing up and being willing to explore.

My subscribers for reading my monthly musings.

Michaela Baker and Ali Squires for loyal and much appreciated business support.

Contents

Foreword

If ever there was a time for this book then it's most definitely now. Throughout the world remuneration structures for financial advisers are becoming increasingly transparent. More and more countries are moving to a fee-only world and that means one thing: advisers need to deliver value. Real value.

In the old days, in a world of smoke and mirrors, in a world of commission, when clients thought financial advice was 'free', when they didn't really know or understand what they were paying for in financial advice, advisers got away with a traditional product and an investment-focused 'transactional' service. But not anymore. Now more than ever, advisers need to deliver real demonstrable value, not just in year one, but year after year, after year. Otherwise, it's only a matter of time before clients question their fees.

Add to this the increasing 'savviness' of consumers and an environment in which direct-to-customer offerings are becoming more commonplace, and more and more enticing, with simple, easy-to-use technology enabling consumers to buy and manage their own financial products online in a matter of minutes, and it becomes clear that the life of the traditional financial adviser is limited. For advisers who only offer a service that revolves around financial products or investments, it's certainly time to wake up.

Depressing? Far from it. There are limitless opportunities for advisers who can engage with clients at a more meaningful level; who can find out what it is that clients really want; who can inspire and encourage clients to live a life of their dreams; to help them get what they most want out of life before it's too late; who can deliver a genuinely client-focused service.

Now more than ever, people are lonely. They crave attention. Just look at the success of Facebook! People are screaming out 'Be interested in me!' But the sad reality of today's fast-paced world is that most people are too busy – or too distracted – to be interested in anybody but themselves. Customer service from many traditional institutions is dead. Relationships with most suppliers are shallow at best. It seems nobody cares.

But then you walk in, you ask great questions and you listen. Attentively. You demonstrate that you are sincerely interested in another human being. You are interested in their story. Where are they now? How did they get to where they are and where are they trying to get to? What do they want to do, be or have in the time they've got left on this planet? What's most important to them and why? What would need to happen in order to have a life well lived?

Engaging with clients at a deeper level is what this book is all about. Not touchy-feely. Just down-to-earth, practical, proven methods of engaging with clients at a deeper level, with the intention to serve. To help them get what they want most – a life well-lived, financial independence, financial security and real peace of mind. That's what everybody wants – they might just not be able to convey it without your help. Our job, as advisers, is to uncover what clients really want and then help them to get it. In this book, John Dashfield shows you how.

Paul Armson
Founder – Inspiring Advisers
www.InspiringAdvisers.co.uk

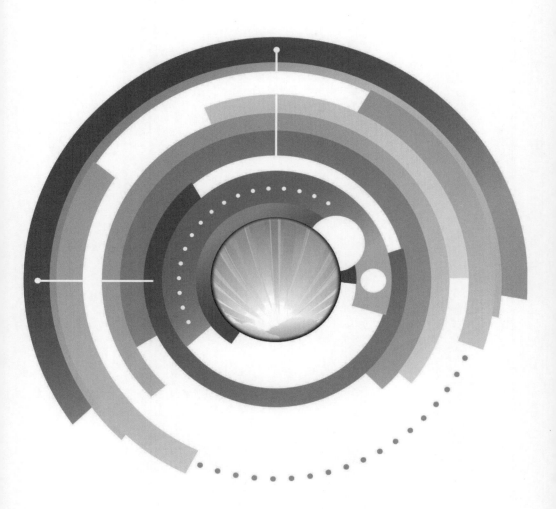

Introduction

Introduction

Think of how you might describe your very best and most rewarding client relationships – inspiring, collaborative, responsive, warm and, of course, profitable.

What if all your client relationships could be like this or even better? What if building your practice could be easier, less stressful and more enjoyable than ever before?

From your client's perspective, how much do you think they would value their relationship with you if it genuinely helped them realise more of their potential and get more of the life they really want?

Financial services is and always will be a people business

Despite the fact that practitioners have been fed a diet of almost nothing but technical information for a long time, at its very core, being a financial services practitioner is far more than simply fulfilling a technical role.

At its best, it is about connecting with clients in a deeply human way. It is about helping individuals, families and businesses to make intelligent and wise financial decisions. It is about helping people live authentic lives that align with what matters most to them. It is about helping people have a healthy relationship with their finances. Although it is a fact that often seems to get pushed into the background, it is about professional people caring for their clients with the utmost integrity and making a genuinely positive difference to their lives.

What clients will value most is your ability to relate to them, connect with them and be curious enough to do what it takes to understand them deeply. They want you to listen to them, reassure them, tell the truth, help them gain clarity and help them feel confident about the future. They want to trust you completely and feel they are in safe hands.

This book will introduce you to the most significant factor in becoming a truly client-centred adviser and building a client-centred practice. We will go deeper than just focusing upon skills, tactics and techniques and explore something far more fundamental to your performance. This factor is at the very core of how quickly, how well and how deeply you build exceptionally high-quality client relationships. In fact, it is at the core of exceptional performance in everything that you do and yet it is a factor that is often invisible to us, overlooked and misunderstood.

It is easier than you think

There is a common misunderstanding in the business world that results come purely from our actions and behaviours. As a coach, the question I hear most often from people when they want to accomplish better results is 'What do I need to do?'

This question, although asked innocently and with good intentions, often fails to help. Far more important than what we do is the state of mind we are doing it in because behaviour emanates from state of mind. How often do we ask ourselves 'Who do I need to be to get the results I want?'

Your ability to build exceptionally high-trust, genuine heartfelt connection and understanding with people, make good decisions and be highly effective in whatever you choose to do is entirely state-of-mind related. When you have a clear and present state of mind you are free to perform at your very best. However, rather than something that involves effort to achieve, mental clarity is your natural state. Often, all we really need to know is how to get out of our own way.

This book is presented in four sections:

Section 1 – The state-of-mind factor

In this first section we will look at the state-of-mind factor and why it is the most critical factor in your performance and, therefore, your results. We will look at the science behind states of mind and how this understanding, rather than any kind of practice or technique, is what leads to higher psychological functioning and increased wellbeing. This understanding, as I know from my own personal experience and my work with my clients over the last few years, is often transformational.

Section 2 – Building client-centred relationships

We will then look at the essential core elements of building exceptionally high-quality client-centred relationships and facilitating deep client engagement. Instead of adopting a technique-based perspective, we will explore each element from a state-of-mind perspective, which will give you a much deeper grounding from which to consistently create exceptionally high-quality relationships. For instance, although most of us probably consider ourselves to be good listeners, we will explore a new way of listening that will significantly deepen and enhance your client relationships. We will also explore the art of client-centred questioning with lots of examples of powerful questions you can use with your clients.

Section 3 – Masters at work: five successful client-centred practitioners share their philosophy

In this section you will read the individual contributions of five successful client-centred advisers. Each has a unique business and approach and yet all of them create exceptionally strong, productive and profitable client-centred relationships. This will give you practical examples of what we are talking about in the earlier chapters.

Section 4 – New client engagement

In this final section of the book we will explore the core elements of new client engagement. Rather than being the chore that many practitioners find, you will discover that by putting the client right at the centre, building your practice becomes easy and enjoyable.

Your biggest leverage point

Throughout the book we will go much deeper than simply focusing on what to do because whilst prescriptive solutions can be interesting, and sometimes helpful, they are not your biggest leverage point.

I have found that simply giving people information rarely, if ever, helps them. If someone just wants to know how to do something, then they can simply google it. This book points you in the direction of your own extraordinary potential and gives you the understanding to unlock it.

Does it work?

For many years I had been coaching my clients using a variety of tools, techniques and systems based around practical psychology, such as neurolinguistic programming. Whilst the results had been excellent I noticed that people, myself included, could still succumb to periods of poor performance and difficulty and it seemed as though I did not yet have the complete answer to what was going on.

Then a few years ago, quite by chance, I came across a new paradigm in psychology and it was obvious that people who were developing an understanding of this paradigm for themselves were experiencing profoundly positive changes in their lives. They were happier, more engaged with life, more productive, far less stressed and bounced back far more quickly from setbacks.

I wanted to learn as much as I could about this new paradigm and, initially, I spent an intense few months, travelling to California and back home again six times, spending hours and hours in classes, reading books and receiving coaching from some of the best state-of-mind practitioners in the world.

I immediately began to share this new paradigm with my clients and they found the same as me. Life becomes far more effortless, enjoyable and yet more productive. Whilst none of us can escape or avoid difficulties, challenges and setbacks, having access to much greater levels of resilience makes them much, much less of an issue.

One of my clients sent me a list of his results and with his permission I have printed his email to me here:

> They often say 'the proof of the pudding… etc.' So I wanted to let you know about some significant improvements since engaging with you.
>
> 1. I have a different approach putting the client first and trying to understand the 'personal' goal behind the goal.
> 2. I have passed my taxation course with a merit.
> 3. I have charged my first £250 monthly fee.
> 4. I have asked clients for testimonials and received some great responses.
> 5. This has put me in the top 100 rated advisers in the UK.

6. *This has provided four new and quality clients in a week.*

7. *I have freed up time by investing in a paraplanner.*

8. *I turned away a client as I wasn't prepared to act transactionally.*

9. *I have significantly improved my approach with clients, telling them how I work, no longer being needy.*

10. *I have significantly improved my confidence to ask for fees.*

11. *I have increased my trail and seen it grow significantly.*

12. *I have reduced my debt, feel better and am enjoying working in the present.*

After teaching and coaching this understanding to my one-to-one clients I felt inspired to share it with a wider audience. The outcome is this book, which will demystify where high-performance comes from and help you create a rewarding client-centred practice.

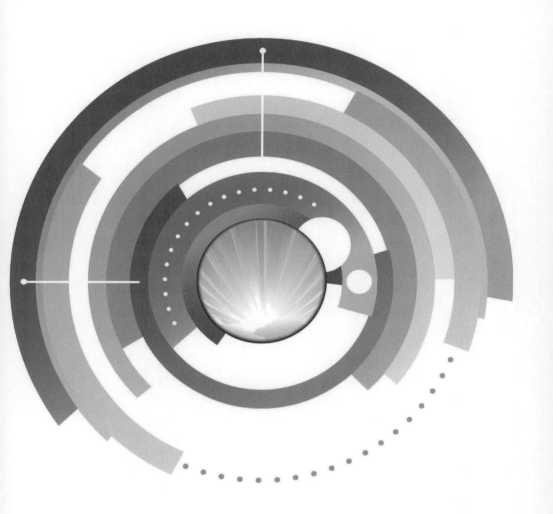

How to get the most
from this book

How to get the most from this book

To help you get the most out of this book I am going to ask you to read it a little differently to how you might normally read business-related material.

You are most likely to be used to reading business content in an intellectual way. This simply means reading to understand and remember it and, as a financial professional, you have almost certainly done a lot of this kind of reading in the past because you have needed to absorb information to make sense of technical material, pass exams and obtain your qualifications.

One of the ways we try to make sense of new ideas is by associating them with existing ideas or knowledge that we already have, however, with this book I would ask you to avoid doing this.

It will be of most help to you to approach this material with an open mind and by letting go of the need to attach it or to compare it to what you already know. This will help you tremendously with absorbing the ideas in a way that will give you the most benefit.

The way to read this book is as you would read a novel. Just read in a relaxed manner, be open-minded and enjoy it.

You will notice a certain amount of repetition throughout the book. This is intentional as seeing the core principles in a variety of different ways and in different contexts will help you to have more of your own insights, fresh thinking and new ideas.

The terms used in this book

I use the terms 'practitioner', 'financial adviser', 'adviser', 'financial professional' or 'planner' interchangeably throughout. I am making no distinction between these terms.

When using the terms 'state of mind' and 'quality of mind' I am referring to our moment-by-moment experience of our thoughts and feelings.

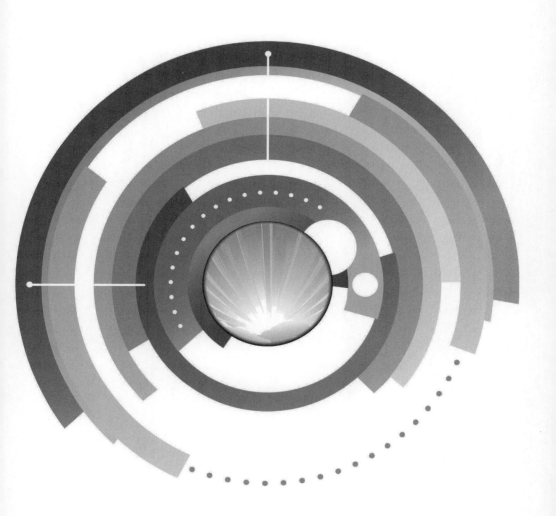

Section 1

The state-of-mind factor

Chapter 1

**Making the
invisible visible**

Chapter 1 – Making the invisible visible

If you have built castles in the air, your work need not be lost; that is where they should be. Now put the foundations under them. **Henry David Thoreau**

Money is a means value. It is simply a means to an end rather than an end in itself. It is what we can do with the money or what the money can do for us that are important and yet the majority of the financial services profession seems to focus entirely upon the means rather than the end.

Financial practitioners are comfortable talking about products, investments or financially based problems. However, they are often uncomfortable having conversations that engage clients in an emotional way about what matters most to them in life, and so avoid having them.

You may have spent scores, possibly hundreds, of hours gaining your technical knowledge and qualifications and, of course, it is vitally important that you are able to give high-quality advice, but how can any practitioner give highly relevant, clear and specific client-centred planning and advice without knowing who the client is, what really matters to them in life and what their ultimate goals, objectives and outcomes are? Without connecting with your client in a human way, so that they articulate, as much for themselves as for you, how they want to live both now and in the future, then how can clear, intelligent decisions be made?

As a practitioner you can be:

- Product and investment centred
- Problem and solution centred
- Client centred

This distinction points to your primary intention. Is it to sell or provide products and investments? Is it to solve financial problems? Or is it to have a deep human connection and thorough understanding of your client and what they want from life and then to collaborate in accomplishing what is most important to them?

To be a truly client-centred financial professional requires far more than technical know-how. It requires you to be willing to do what it takes to know how your clients want to live their lives. Only by doing this can you integrate someone's finances into a meaningful plan and strategy that links directly into what they want from life. Of course, arranging products and solving financial problems is also part of what a client-centred adviser does, but these are not primary tasks because they are simply a vehicle rather than the destination.

Being truly client centred is the most viable long-term, high-reward, business model because it creates more, not less, opportunity for you. When clients absolutely know that you have their very best interests at heart because they can feel where you are coming from then there are multiple benefits:

- They will entrust you with more of their money.
- They see incredible value in the work you do together.
- They hold you and your advice, recommendations and input in the very highest regard.
- They willingly pay your fees without quibble.
- They become totally loyal to you.
- They refer you to other like-minded people.

The landscape has changed

If we go back in time 40 or 50 years or more then life was very linear. People went to school, maybe on to further education or an apprenticeship, then got a job and were highly likely to be in that job for life before eventual retirement. It was all about stability.

Modern life is totally different. It is unpredictable and the only constant is change. We are likely to have several careers. We are far more mobile. We are likely to go through several significant life transitions. More and more of us are resisting the idea of traditional retirement and, instead, want to travel, start a business or have another career. We want fulfilment and a satisfying life experience.

People's finances are right at the heart of living an authentic life that aligns with who they want to be and how they want to live. They need and want support, but the right kind of support. They want a financial adviser who knows who they are and that they can trust 100 per cent to put their interests first and give relevant, practical and wise guidance. They do not want someone who is only interested in selling them something or talking technical jargon to them.

You cannot compete on cost, so what is the alternative?

The development of technology has driven costs right down and is making online transactions easier and more attractive. You cannot hope to compete on cost, which is why being a product-centred or a problem- and solution-centred practitioner will only yield ever-diminishing returns. This is not something that will happen in the future; it is happening right now and the evidence is crystal clear in many ways, for example, low cost products, the rise of comparison websites and services from providers cut to the bone so that your business bears more of the cost. The only viable option left open to you is to deliver such high value that your fees are seen as a worthwhile investment rather than a cost.

The client-centred adviser understands this new dynamic. They see that what clients want is someone who is truly interested in them. They know that the real value for the client is not in the transaction; it is in having powerful conversations. Any practitioner can sell a financial product and because the general level of practitioner's technical proficiency is becoming higher and higher then this cannot differentiate you either. What you have left is you. It is when you show up as a powerful person, an inspiring person, a person who is willing to hold your client to a higher standard, that you create a transformational rather than a transactional experience for your clients.

What you read in this book will help you to effortlessly put the client right at the very centre of what you do and position you and your business for present and long-term success. You will discover something far more lasting, valuable and impactful than just another bunch of techniques because it goes right to the very core of who you are being.

The state-of-mind factor

Right at the very heart of being a truly client-centred adviser is your state of mind. It is not just another factor, it is *the* factor. Your state of mind affects, more than anything else, the experience that your clients have. For example, if you feel self-orientated, under pressure or distracted then this will significantly lower the quality of your meetings and client relationships.

Conversely, when you are functioning at a high psychological level you can facilitate client meetings that deliver enormous value because your clients experience them as inspiring, uplifting, insightful, collaborative and creative.

A clear mind enables you to be deeply curious, listen without judgement, ask appropriate, high-quality questions and have no personal agenda. This leads to a deep bond of trust with your client and elicits very high-quality information so that your subsequent advice perfectly aligns with what is most important to your client. In the next chapter we will look at the science behind what creates state of mind but before doing this let us look at just some of the differences between healthy and unhealthy psychological functioning.

Healthy psychological functioning	Unhealthy psychological functioning
Clarity of mind	Distracted by own thinking
At ease	Tense, anxious, worried
Builds rapport easily	Difficulty in building meaningful rapport
Feels secure	Feels insecure
Intuitive	Closed up
Low self-orientation	High self-orientation
Connects in a human way	Aloof or disconnected
Curious	Focused on running own agenda
Listens exceptionally well to others	Poor listener, consumed by own thinking
Creative	Bereft of ideas
Resilient	Takes things personally

Healthy psychological functioning	Unhealthy psychological functioning
Trusting	Controlling, overly concerned with outcome
Low error and mistake rate	Higher error and mistake rate
Exercises good judgement	Prone to lapses in judgement

Every activity and aspect of life that we can engage in is going to be deeply affected by our level of psychological functioning. When we are in clear and present states of mind then all of our best qualities are naturally available and we are free to perform exceptionally well.

In professional sports this is completely understood. A player's level of psychological functioning is recognised as a critical factor in success as much as physical conditioning, skills and tactical know-how. In fact, it is an athlete's healthy psychological functioning that links everything together. The ultimate edge that exceptional performers have is a psychological one and athletes routinely employ a coach to help them with the mental side of their game.

In business, state of mind often remains invisible or is dismissed as having little relevance. Even when recognised as a factor, approaches to improvement often have a poor record of success because they are based upon theory rather than clear principles.

In your work as a practitioner a healthy, high-functioning state of mind is essential to creating meaningful, high-trust relationships. If we were to take just some of the key capabilities required to build client-centred relationships, all of them are either empowered or disempowered by your state of mind. You will read about these in much greater detail further into the book but just consider for a moment what some of these key capabilities are:

- Building deep trust and rapport quickly
- Making clients feel comfortable about talking about what can be difficult subjects
- Guiding your clients into clear, insightful thinking
- Deep listening
- Intelligent questioning
- Demonstrating that you understand your client
- Having the humility that encourages clients to really listen to you
- Keeping your clients highly engaged throughout the whole planning process and into the future

When we are in low-functioning states of mind all of these qualities are far less available to us, if at all. The lower our state of mind the lower our ability to relate to other people. Often, because low states of mind have become habitual over a long period of time, many people do not even realise how low their functioning has been until it starts to improve. The only thing they know is that they feel under pressure, things seem difficult and there is a lack of enjoyment in what they do.

So, what provides a solution?

From my own personal experience and thousands of hours of coaching financial practitioners, business owners and executives, I have seen that what has the most immediate, biggest and lasting impact on performance is a clear understanding of state of mind and what creates it because the by-product of this is healthier psychological functioning.

A shift in understanding

Unless we understand that our level of psychological functioning is by far the biggest factor in our performance it can be easily overlooked. Instead we look for ways to improve that may have only marginal effect or are impaired because we have thinking that works against us.

For example, when it comes to business and personal improvement, the business world is awash with prescriptive techniques that promise to help us get the results that we want. It is easy to imagine that creating client-centred relationships is all about simply learning and adopting some new tools, techniques and capabilities.

However, behaviour is the tip of the iceberg and yet it is often treated as the whole iceberg. The reason that we so often focus upon trying to alter our behaviour is that it is visible. If, for example, we see someone or a system that is getting great results then we may think this must be the answer we are looking for and so we invest in trying to emulate the behaviour. However, behaviour is the *result* of state of mind. It is someone's state of mind that powers everything up; it is like the electricity to the light bulb and this fact is usually missed.

If you reflect upon the earlier comparison between healthy and unhealthy psychological functioning, then imagine trying to adopt new behaviours effectively, especially inter-personal behaviours, whilst in low-functioning psychological states of mind. It is impossible and yet this is what many people are trying to do.

Of course, prescriptive solutions can work for people when they have the state of mind that aligns with the behaviour. However, there are many instances where people find that developing new behaviours is difficult because they have a state of mind that works against them rather than supporting them in their desired outcomes. Paradoxically, when we are in low-functioning states of mind we find prescriptive solutions of little use anyway and when we are in high-functioning states of mind we have access to our own inner resources.

Your core ability as a practitioner

The technical competence of financial professionals has risen significantly due to the requirements for higher qualifications. As mentioned at the beginning of this chapter, most practitioners have spent huge amounts of time in study, however, technical knowledge and qualifications have no correlation whatsoever with inter-personal skills.

Taking a technical approach with clients is highly likely to switch them off. From a client's perspective financial planning is not an analytical, hard fact, number-crunching, linear and technical process. It is a deeply personal, emotional exploration, a time to connect with what matters most and to consider important life decisions. Therefore, the core ability that clients will judge you on is not your technical know-how, it is your ability to connect with them and communicate effectively. It is how you relate to them, put them at ease and facilitate their higher psychological functioning that matters because everything else flows from this.

Being product and investment centred or problem and solution centred will often bypass the opportunity to facilitate powerful, positive, possibly life-changing experiences for your clients because it is self-orientated and fails to put the client right at the very centre. In Sections 2 and 4 of the book we will explore, in a variety of ways, how state of mind plays out in client meetings and in the process of engaging new clients. You will read stories and anecdotes about real situations that I have drawn from my client coaching notes (names changed, of course) and have an opportunity to deepen your understanding of state of mind and what creates it. So that you get the most insight from these sections of the book it is important to have the foundation of the scientific principles behind what creates your state of mind, which we will explore in the next chapter.

Thoughts to reflect on

As a practitioner you can be 'product and investment centred', 'problem and solution centred' or 'client centred'.

Being client centred is the most viable, sustainable and high-reward business model.

Your state of mind is right at the heart of being a client-centred adviser.

Behaviour is the result of state of mind, therefore, new behaviours will only successfully integrate if there is a supportive state of mind.

Your ability to connect in a human way and relate to your clients is what they value the most and has the biggest impact, rather than your technical knowledge.

Chapter 2

The science behind state of mind

Chapter 2 – The science behind state of mind

All truth goes through three steps: first, it is ridiculed; second, it is violently opposed; finally, it is accepted as self-evident. **Arthur Schopenhauer, German philosopher**

Putting your client right at the centre of everything you do and facilitating a rich and meaningful experience for them emerges naturally from a free and present state of mind. In fact, mental clarity is what drives your performance in everything that you do and so experiencing high-functioning states of mind more of the time will positively impact all of your activities and results (see the table in the previous chapter for comparison of healthy/unhealthy psychological functioning).

This being so it would be easy to draw the conclusion that you need to work upon getting your state of mind 'right'. However, there is no work for you to do and it is not necessary to employ any mind management techniques or practices to help rid yourself of unproductive thinking or 'bad' emotional states so that you can function healthily. Quite the opposite, because it is too much mental activity such as overthinking, a busy mind and habits such as worrying that remove our clarity of mind.

It is having an understanding of how the mind really works that opens up your potential to experiencing ever-increasing levels of healthy psychological functioning.

One of the things I have learned, from receiving great coaching myself, and teaching and coaching others, is that just giving people information rarely helps them. The new paradigm of psychology you are about to be introduced to is most easily understood through examples, stories and metaphors. This is the way the book has been designed and written but there needs to be a foundation for it all to make sense.

Approaching with an open mind

We tend to look at life through the lens of our existing beliefs, knowledge and understanding and this is true whenever we begin to learn something new. However, if you are willing to suspend what you already know and be open-minded then you will see that experiencing a healthy state of mind and a high level of psychological functioning is your natural way of being rather than something you have to strive for, work towards or put any effort into experiencing. Nature designed us to function optimally and it is only through a misunderstanding that far too many of us are trying to achieve the results we want whilst suffering with stressed, overburdened and busy states of mind.

The false paradigm

The misunderstanding that almost all of humanity is under is that our feelings are coming from something other than our thought in the moment. We tend to look towards our life conditions, circumstances, situations, events, the past, the future, our relationships, our work, money and, in fact, a long list of possible causes as being responsible for how we feel.

If we are worried about money then we think our feeling has something to do with the money. If we have an issue with another person then we think that they have something to do with how we feel. If we feel under pressure then it looks as if it is because we have stressful circumstances, for instance, too much to do and too little time to do it in.

This false, outside-in, paradigm is why we are so often apt to look to and blame our circumstances for how we feel. When we think that something other than our thinking is responsible for how we feel, then it often leads to behaviour to try to deal with or cope with what we think is the source. For example, we might try to avoid certain circumstances, situations or people. We might be compelled to put a lot of energy into trying to get our circumstances 'right', so we can feel at peace. We might just accept that stress is inherent in what we do and conclude that the best we can do is learn to cope with it or manage it.

This 'outside-in' misunderstanding of how life works is at the very core of all of our difficulties and explains why we can spend far more time than is necessary in low-functioning states of mind.

The truth – the inside-out paradigm and the principle of Thought

The true paradigm of life is that our feelings only ever come from our thought in the moment. We live in a thought/feeling system, meaning that we have a thought and we feel it; you cannot separate the two. The outside world is completely neutral and cannot directly give us a feeling, even though it looks as if it does.

So, if we worry about money our feeling is coming from our thought in the moment about money and has nothing to do with the money. Our issues with other people come from our thought in the moment about the person and have nothing to do with them. If we feel under pressure then it is our thought in the moment about our circumstances, amount of work and lack of time that creates the feeling, not the circumstance.

We have all had the experience of having a difficult problem, seemingly without an obvious solution or acceptable course of action, and yet we have slept on it and by morning we have clarity. What has really changed? It is our thinking.

This inside-out nature of our life experience is a scientific fact, with no exception. From the moment we enter this world to the moment we leave it what we experience from moment to moment is our thinking. The reason this is so often invisible to us is because we are like fish in water; our thinking seems so real to us that it looks as if we are directly experiencing our circumstances.

A thought experiment

Think of an area of a recurring difficulty or problem you experience in your life. Now just reflect for a moment by asking yourself:

*   Are my feelings coming directly from [the difficulty or problem]?
*   Are my feelings coming from my thought in the moment about [the difficulty or problem]?

There can only ever be one true answer. We all know that we think, however, what we do not see, until we have this new understanding, is that our thinking is our entire life.

Why do thoughts seem so real? – The principle of Consciousness

Consciousness, which is really another word for awareness, is how we experience the thoughts that we have. Consciousness is like a flashlight being shone on a thought and, through your senses, it brings a thought to life. Without it we would have no experience of anything and the combination of thought and consciousness is the reason that we can have such powerful feelings associated with particular thoughts and why they look and feel so real to us.

If, for example, you have the thought that your business is going badly, and you really engage with that thought, then your consciousness will bring it to life via the senses. You will experience all the sensations and feelings associated with that particular thought and because such an experience can be so intense it seems as if it is real. This is how we can be fooled by our thoughts into taking action that often proves to be ineffective or even counterproductive. Fearful, insecure and anxious thinking is unreliable. Therefore, a huge implication of seeing the thought/feeling connection is that we stop acting upon this kind of thinking, which alone will raise our game, often significantly, because we make far fewer mistakes and errors of judgement.

Consciousness is bringing us the sensory experience of our thoughts constantly but it also allows us to step back from our thoughts and observe them, which is what allows us to create the choice, through our free will, of whether we give life to a particular thought or not. As our level of consciousness rises we gain greater awareness of our thinking and our relationship to it shifts.

From a higher level of consciousness, you can still have the thought of your business going badly, you can experience all the sensations and the feelings of that thought, but when you know it is a thought and that it is only you giving it life, then you have a choice as to whether it has power over you or not. It is the understanding that does the work for you rather than needing to exert any kind of control over your thoughts.

The principle of Mind

We live in a world of thought, brought alive by consciousness, and we can have only two kinds of thought: a new thought or an old thought.

Our old thoughts are simply ones we have had before and many of these have become thought habits. We think them but we are unaware that we think them and so they are unconsciously influencing our behaviour and responses to life. The vast majority of our fears, worries and anxieties are old, recycled thoughts that, because our consciousness makes them look so real, continue to unsettle us and control our behaviour.

Beyond our recycled, personal, habitual thinking is our innate capacity for new thought. There is an intelligent energy behind life that is the source of innate wisdom, insights, fresh thinking, moments of clarity and creativity. This intelligent energy is known as the principle of Mind.

One way to think about this is that when we are using our memory-based mind it is like using a computer offline; we can only retrieve answers that are stored within the existing data. Sometimes we will have the answer that we need, but what if we don't? A tendency many people have is to keep thinking into their problems trying to grind out an answer but this usually works against us because in this state of mind we lose our capacity for insight or, at the very least, are far less likely to get new thinking. When we relax and appreciate that new thinking comes to a quiet mind, it is like connecting to the internet and the infinite potential for new answers.

This innate intelligence is available to us all of the time and will effortlessly guide us through life when we allow it to. It is the mistaken belief that we have to intellectually think our way through life that creates an unnecessary burden that many of us carry.

We live in a self-clearing system

The human mind is designed to clear itself. If you watch a young child of three or four years old, you can see that they experience a wide range of feelings, positive and negative. When experiencing states such as anger, frustration, sadness, distress or fear you can also notice just how quickly a child returns to the present and mental clarity.

So, how do they do this when, as adults, we can seem to spend so much more of our time in unhealthy psychological states of mind?

The reason that children function optimally is because they do not think about their thinking. They do not make meaning out of their low moods. They can have any thought and feeling, experience it, and then let it go. Many times, when my children were little, I could watch them have a tantrum, get frustrated or sad over something and yet, within minutes, their mind would clear and they would be totally immersed in something else.

Becoming high functioning far more of the time is not about trying to control your thoughts, which is impossible. Just try it for any length of time if you doubt this. It is about having an understanding of how we live in a thought-created reality and that all thoughts are neutral, unless we give life to them.

We are only ever one thought away from clarity

The three principles of Mind, Thought and Consciousness, the gift given to us by the late Sydney Banks, work together in creating our experience of life moment by moment. They are principles because, like all principles, they are constant, unchanging and work all the time without exception, whether you know about them or not. It is challenging even to articulate them because, just like the principle of gravity, although we can see the effects the principles themselves have no form.

Right at the very heart of your effectiveness as a client-centred adviser and as a person is the quality of your psychological functioning. These principles explain where our experience is coming from. They are not a technique or a method, they are like the operating system of the human mind, and by developing an understanding and an appreciation of them it creates greater awareness, choice and access to our innate intelligence.

None of us has to be controlled by our old, erroneous and habitual thinking. We do not need to feel fearful, insecure or afraid. Perfect wellbeing is how we came into this world and is only ever one thought away. As we reorientate ourselves from believing our circumstances are responsible for our feelings to understanding the inside-out nature of life, then we begin to spend more and more time experiencing mental clarity and wellbeing, which has profound implications for our performance, results and overall experience of life.

In the next chapter we will explore how mental clarity impacts the bottom line of your business and is the core factor in sharpening your improvement curve.

Thoughts to reflect on

Understanding how the mind really works opens up your potential to experiencing ever-increasing levels of healthy psychological functioning.

Our feelings are coming from our thought in the moment, even though it so often looks as if they come from our circumstances.

Thoughts can seem so vivid and real because consciousness brings them to life.

We have an innate, in-built capacity for new thinking, insight, flashes of inspiration, moments of clarity and creativity.

As we reorientate from the false 'outside-in' paradigm to the true 'inside-out' paradigm our performance will naturally and effortlessly rise because we spend more time in mental wellbeing.

Chapter 3

Being is the new doing

Chapter 3 – Being is the new doing

We cannot solve our problems with the same level of thinking that created them.
Albert Einstein

Ben was an established practitioner who wanted to move his practice from being a product-centred business to a client-centred business. Historically, he had been conducting mostly transactional business and his goal was to spend more time with his clients, focus on helping them accomplish their most important life goals and delegate the majority of the administrative, planning and research work to others.

Whilst the end goal was clear and he had made some good progress over the previous couple of years, Ben was finding the transition stressful. His mind was so busy trying to think it all through that he was finding it difficult to really connect with his clients in a meaningful way, he was struggling with the finer details of how he wanted his practice to run and he was not communicating effectively with his team, which sometimes created friction.

To Ben, the transition to the kind of business he really wanted seemed fraught with difficulty, he often felt discouraged and his confidence was low. Even though he was committed to making the changes, he had resigned himself to the fact that 'this is just how it is'.

I expect, in our own way, we have all had this kind of experience. We want to make positive changes and yet the road ahead seems to be paved with obstacles. But what if change could be easy, effortless and enjoyable?

The myth of change

A question that I often ask my clients when we first meet is 'What are the things standing in the way of your business becoming a much better business?'

I am curious about what they think the obstacles are and, as you can probably imagine, people's answers vary in content but they often relate to needing some kind of process improvement. I have never once had anyone say 'state of mind' because, as we saw in Chapter 1, state of mind is either invisible to us or dismissed as being a significant factor.

However, it is important to realise that in the process of building a client-centred business there are two crucial components:

- State-of-mind improvement
- Process improvement

Clearly, building a much better business involves the creation, improvement and implementation of effective processes. However, without understanding the state-of-mind factor the result can be that process improvement is impaired, slow and perceived as difficult because we are going about it in states of mind that hinder rather than help us get where we want to go. Also, every business has a culture, whether intentionally created or not, because culture is the collective state of mind of the people in the business. When people's state of mind improves, the culture will improve by itself, which results in better teamwork, problem solving and client focus.

To Ben, it looked as though his feelings of stress and difficulty were coming directly from the experience of trying to grow and evolve his practice, rather than his thinking. Consequently, he felt that his only option was to keep grinding away until he was out the other side. In his mind 'the other side' was quite some way off and this was why he felt so discouraged because he thought he was in a no-win situation. He certainly did not want to go backwards so the only option was to keep ploughing on.

Creating sustainable change is one of the biggest challenges for businesses because people do not realise that what they are really up against is their own thinking. The consequence of this is that the approach to change is often one of brute force or force of will. We want to create success for ourselves and so we can think we have to try harder, work longer hours and punish ourselves into improving results.

For example, if we cannot get the result we want in 40 hours a week then we think we have to work 50, 60 or 70 hours. However, this is a model of diminishing returns because there are only so many hours in the day and we can only work so hard before there is no more improvement, things plateau or even decline. If we begin to burn out through exhaustion or discouragement it is counterproductive and yet this is what is going on in many businesses.

This is also how the myth that change is slow, difficult and full of problems perpetuates. If we are overthinking, feeling under pressure and preoccupied with our problems and it looks as though our circumstances are the cause, then it is always going to look as if a change of circumstances is the only solution to feeling better.

How do you sharpen the improvement curve?

I was once fortunate enough to listen to the very successful CEO of a large global company describe how, when he first took the position, the company was failing badly. They were incredibly behind upon the fulfilment of contracts, there were a lot of poor decisions being made and there was a blame culture in which no one was taking responsibility for what was going on.

The company was fully resourced, had hired the best talent money could buy and the CEO had tried all of the strategies, tactics and know-how he had used successfully in the past, but to no avail.

Eventually, the CEO, even though he was sceptical, spoke with a consultant he knew who specialised in teaching the principles behind state of mind. With nothing to lose the organisation began a programme that became known as 'the state-of-mind programme' and the workforce was taught, from the leadership down, the principles behind how the mind works, as described in the previous chapter. This was all the training that was given, so no further skills training, no management training or any other kind of improvement training, just state of mind.

The CEO said that before the programme he was asked by the company providing the programme 'How would twice the productivity, with half the effort and none of the stress sound to you?' He said it sounded like a used-car salesman's pitch and yet he could feel that there was something in what he was hearing and he was willing to take a leap of faith.

This programme was introduced 20 years ago, in the mid 1990s, and the results are legendary, with the organisation going through a long, sustained and continual period of high growth, innovation and success. The blame culture dissolved, people collaborated effectively and the problems were overcome. They also went from an unsustainable level of employee turnover to almost zero. People loved working there.

Effectively, the company went from being very self-consumed to becoming very client centred. As the state of mind and general wellbeing of the workforce improved their attention just naturally turned to doing the very best they could for their clients and producing outstanding work.

When asked what he thought the main factor in this improvement was the CEO said that his people had become 'discouragement-proof'. Through understanding state of mind and what creates it the workforce became incredibly resilient, innovative and inspired.

Achieving your potential

A useful formula and way to think about how to realise more of your and your team's ultimate potential is defined by coach and author Timothy Gallwey (1997) as follows:

Performance = Potential – Interference

Your performance and, therefore, your results will always be defined by your pure potential minus interference. Interference can be broadly defined as unhelpful thinking. For example, stress, worry, anxiety, tension, insecurity, uncertainty or discouragement.

The fact is that we can experience mental clarity and high levels of psychological functioning under any circumstances because, as we saw in the previous chapter, there is no direct link between circumstances and how we feel.

The power of presence

We feel our thinking about our circumstances, we do not feel our circumstances directly. What the inside-out understanding does is pull us back into the present, rather than being consumed by our unhelpful thinking. This has a profoundly positive effect upon our performance.

Any kind of overthinking, internal pressure or stress takes us out of the present moment because what we are paying attention to is our thinking rather than what is in front of us. As so many of us spend a lot of time in unhelpful thinking we forget just how much difference having a clear mind and being fully present really makes.

What does it *really* mean to be fully present?

Rather than being something mysterious or something to aim for, being present is, in fact, very ordinary. I used to think of being present as having something to do with the linear progression of time, as in the past, the present and the future. Then about three years ago I had a powerful insight when I realised that being present had nothing to do with what I had been thinking at all. The experience of being fully present is the deep feeling of inner peace and wellbeing that we have when our mind is free from the distraction of our personal, habitual thinking.

This feeling of presence is a highly significant factor in our performance and is well documented as such. An example of presence is the state of 'flow'. In the early 1990s psychologist Mihaly Csikszentmihalyi wrote a book of the same name, which presented his long-term research into high-performance states. Being in 'flow' is typified by feelings of joy, creativity, higher consciousness, timelessness and a sense of total involvement. Timothy Gallwey wrote a whole series of best-seller 'inner game' books, where he teaches that overthinking and trying too hard is what produces inner tension and conflict and lowers performance.

The people who are most present of all are young children and in the previous chapter we looked at how children function optimally because they do not think about their thinking. They feel their thoughts but, instead of getting caught up in judging their thinking they simply feel it, their mind clears and they get new thoughts. This is the potential that we all have once we see the principles behind our experience.

Being present with your work

Let's go back to Ben, who we met at the beginning of this chapter. Once he began to see for himself that it was his thinking that was creating his feeling, rather than his circumstances, his mind naturally began to settle and clear. Consequently, his decision-making became much better, his relationships improved and he began to enjoy his work again. He had this observation:

> *I had forgotten just how much difference a change of mind makes. I had been feeling overburdened for so long that it began to look like reality to me. As a business, we still have challenges ahead but I am no longer fazed by them and am actually happy taking one day at a time. I am finding I am getting far more done and get to go home earlier too!*

Being present in your client meetings

In our culture we hugely over value 'doing' and hugely under value 'being'. In your client meetings nothing is more powerful than you being fully present. As we showed in Chapter 1, your ability to put your client right at the centre, build high trust, listen without judgement and overall, facilitate a powerful experience for them is most influenced by your degree of presence. When you are present it will pull your clients into this state too. From here they will do their very best thinking and, consequently, they will see enormous value in the time you spend together.

A useful question to reflect on is 'Who do my clients really want me to be?'

Do they want someone showing up who is over-burdened, busy-minded and tense or do they want someone who is deeply in their own wellbeing? Leading coach and author, Steve Chandler (2006) said 'People are attracted to people who own their lives. People are not attracted to victims.'

Being is the new doing

We are so focused upon doing because it can seem as if this is the most efficient way to make progress and yet so much of our 'doing' emerges from fear-based states of mind, such as worry, anxiety or neediness. We think that if we are not busy then we are being unproductive.

However, when we sacrifice being present for being frenetic we so often waste vast amounts of our time and energy as well as bypassing the potential for deep human connection with the people around us, including our clients, our team and our loved ones.

One of the most powerful realisations that people have when they live far more in the present is that life flows easily and effortlessly. Whenever we feel that life is a struggle it is a sign that our thinking is 'off', rather than having anything directly to do with our circumstances. This is the time to check in and ask ourselves where our feeling is coming from because as soon as we see the thought/feeling connection we return to clarity of mind.

In the next section of the book we will explore the core elements of creating client-centred relationships, building on the foundations of healthy psychological functioning and the operating principles of the human mind.

Thoughts to reflect on

The two crucial components in building a much better business are state-of-mind improvement and process improvement.

A better state of mind, both individually and collectively, will sharpen the business improvement curve. Clear thinking enables better decision-making, improved problem solving and increased performance.

Your actual performance equals your pure potential minus interference (unhelpful thinking).

It is useful to reflect on the question 'Who do my clients really want me to be?'

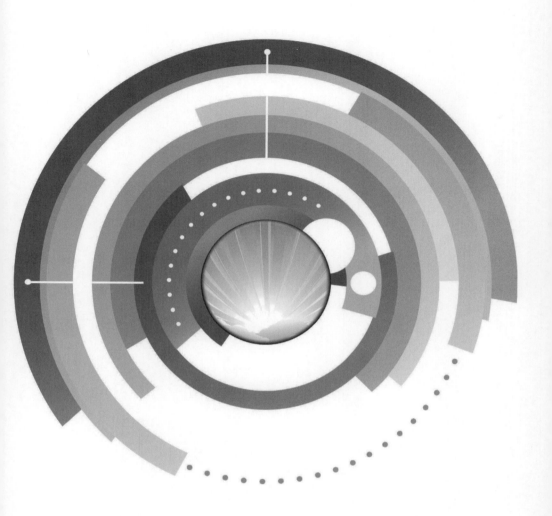

Section 2

Building client-centred relationships

Chapter 4

The three levels of relationship

Chapter 4 – The three levels of relationship

Self-absorption in all its forms kills empathy, let alone compassion. When we focus on ourselves, our world contracts as our problems and preoccupations loom large. But when we focus on others, our world expands. Our own problems drift to the periphery of the mind and so seem smaller, and we increase our capacity for connection – or compassionate action. **Daniel Goleman**

There is a story I once heard about the American company, Southwest Airlines, and how they went about recruiting new cabin crew. Instead of having each applicant come in for an individual interview, what they did was have a larger group of new applicants attend one big interview session. When all the applicants arrived they found they were in a hall with a stage up at the front. Each applicant was asked, in turn, to go up onto the stage and tell the audience a little about themselves and why they wanted the position.

Naturally, what the applicants thought was that they were being judged upon their performance in front of the group. But they were mistaken because the recruitment people were actually observing the audience. What the recruitment people were interested in was how each applicant in the audience was responding to the person on the stage. Who was empathising? Who showed concern? Who genuinely cared?

The airline's thinking was that those people who showed genuine empathy, concern and caring for other people, even in a pressured situation, were likely to make the best cabin crew. They wanted people who naturally focused upon the needs of others without being told to.

The approach was very successful because the crew recruited through that programme received the least complaints and the highest number of compliments compared to crew recruited by traditional methods.

This ability to focus primarily upon serving the needs and requirements of clients is equally important in financial services where creating a deep human connection with your clients is central to the depth of the relationships you build and the quality of the work that you do together.

Your focus of attention within the relationship is critical to how it develops, so it is important to consider how relationships can be created on one of three basic levels.

Level one

At level one the relationship is all about you. Your focus is upon what you are getting out of it, so it is a relationship based upon taking.

Level two

At level two the relationship is about meeting the needs of the other person as well as your own needs. It is a relationship based upon give and take.

Level three

At level three the relationship is totally focused upon meeting the needs of the client. It is a relationship based upon giving.

Southwest Airlines were recruiting people who naturally inclined to have relationships at level three. They wanted to avoid hiring cabin crew who were primarily focused upon themselves because they knew that this would have implications that were out of line with the customer experience they wanted to create. They did not want to employ people whose initial response to a situation was 'How does this affect me?'

Adviser and client relationships

In financial services, adviser and client relationships can exist on any one of those three levels. Historically, the financial services business has attracted a significant amount of criticism because it has been considered to be self-serving and, in many instances, has failed to put the interests of the client first. So, clearly, it is not desirable to create relationships at level one.

At first glance it can make sense for relationships to exist at level two because if both parties are getting their needs met then what is wrong with that? In fact, it is true that many adviser and client relationships do exist at this level.

However, these kinds of relationship are transactional in nature. From the adviser's perspective the relationship will feel superficial and, often, there will be little more depth to the relationship than there would be with a retailer. Of course, it can be cordial, polite and friendly but it falls way short of the potential, which can only be fulfilled within a level three relationship.

The very highest standard of relationship between the adviser and client exists at level three. To do your best work, truly impact people and have your advice and guidance held in the very highest regard then the relationship can only be at this level. At all times it can *only* be about your clients and can *only* be completely transparent. Importantly, from the practitioner's perspective, level three relationships are far more enriching and meaningful. Paradoxically, by unconditionally focusing upon the needs of others, there are significant commercial benefits such as producing bigger cases, more repeat business and more referrals.

Creating high-trust level three relationships

There is a considerable amount of information available on how to create high-trust business relationships and most of it focuses upon skills and behaviour, i.e. what you need to do to win trust. For example, the advice is often given that to build trust you need to listen to people, understand them and show genuine care.

However, as we discovered in Section 1, behaviour is a by-product of state of mind. You can teach people all the skills and behaviours in the world but without the quality of mind to bring them to life it will make little or no difference. For example, people can receive training in communication skills but the effective utilisation of those skills is absolutely dependent upon state of mind. When an adviser feels insecure, under pressure or self-absorbed this will significantly impair their ability to connect meaningfully with other people.

Creating high-trust business relationships is about the quality of mind that you bring to the relationship. When you feel secure within yourself and therefore, able to focus entirely upon serving your client, then all the behaviours that are associated with creating exceptionally high trust are a natural by-product. The human touch, which is what really deepens trust and connection between people, is created when you have a completely clear mind, rather than by employing techniques or trying to 'do' trustworthiness.

What bringing a clear mind to your client relationships means is:

- You are fully present in your client meetings and able to give your complete attention.
- You easily develop deep rapport.
- You listen well and without judgement.
- You have insightful, intuitive thinking.
- You feel comfortable asking challenging questions.
- Your communication is far more powerful.

In Chapter 2, we explored the link between thought and feeling that naturally brings us back to the present and a clear mind. From here, high-quality relationships develop easily and naturally, without having to try.

What undermines relationships?

Ultimately, what weakens, undermines and contaminates any relationship is negative thinking, which could be in the form of complacency, blame, neediness, controlling behaviour or a lack of attention. What all these arise from are feelings of insecurity.

Feeling insecure leads to self-orientation and this will negatively influence the dynamic of a relationship. Quite how insecurity shows up will vary enormously from person to person. One of the most common ways is being a 'people pleaser', which will get in the way of having powerful client relationships.

The 'people pleaser' is always doing things to be helpful and to keep people happy, which on the face of it seems to make sense, but when this behaviour is being driven by insecurity because we want to be liked, avoid being turned down, or are hoping for reciprocation (e.g. getting someone's business), it weakens the relationship. For example, the practitioner may be reluctant to ask searching questions or sidestep 'difficult' issues through fear of a negative reaction from the client and, therefore, the potential to serve someone more deeply is lost.

Another way that insecurity shows up is being overly concerned with the outcome of a meeting. This can show up in many ways but rigidly trying to stick to a process, trying to evaluate how a meeting is going or thinking about the business you might get are all distractions that will have a detrimental effect upon the relationship.

Karen's story

Karen is a successful financial planner who is the perfect example of someone who has high-quality, level three relationships. She is confident, intuitive and totally committed to helping her clients accomplish what is most important to them and lead high-quality lives.

When meeting a new client Karen has no agenda other than to connect with and deeply understand them because she knows that this is the foundation of a productive relationship. She sees herself as performing several roles with her clients. She is a planner, a coach and she holds her clients accountable. For example, she may see that some of her clients have poor habits with money, which, if left to continue could compromise the accomplishment of their goals. So, if she sees behaviour from a client that is out of line with their goals, for example continual overspending, she will pick this up with them and is not afraid to create tension because she can see the bigger picture. Her clients instinctively know and feel that she is totally on their side and if Karen is robust in her questioning they appreciate it because of where she is coming from.

Karen's business is built upon referrals and introduction. People want to work with her because she helps them get the results that really matter to them. By working with her they feel more secure, have more peace of mind and less worry, which are the very kind of outcomes that improve someone's quality of life.

If Karen were working only at level two then her relationships would be created completely differently. If her attention was on what she was getting out of the situation then people would feel this and be unlikely to feel comfortable to really open up or be challenged. At best, it would reduce the relationship to a transactional one and lose the tremendous mutual upside potential gained through level three relationships.

There is always the potential to deepen any relationship and be of greater service to someone, no matter how good you think the relationship currently is. It is useful to reflect on your own client relationships and where you think they currently are. How are you showing up in your client relationships? What are your opportunities to be of greater service? How can you enhance the lives of your clients even more?

Thoughts to reflect on

Level one relationships are about taking; level two relationships are about give and take; level three relationships are all about giving.

Your client relationships can only be based upon giving, if they are to be of the highest quality.

Your quality of mind will determine the level of the relationships that you create.

What undermines any relationship are feelings of insecurity.

You don't need to focus upon techniques to gain trust. When you have a clear and present mind trust and rapport are a natural by-product.

Chapter 5

A new way of listening

Chapter 5 – A new way of listening

Good listeners have a huge advantage. For one, when they engage in conversation, they make people 'feel' heard. They 'feel' that someone really understands their wants, needs and desires. And for good reason; a good listener does care to understand.
Simon Sinek

My experience is that most, if not all, financial practitioners would say they are good listeners. Many say so in their practice's literature and on their website. However, there is another level of listening beyond what most people are familiar with that will add a new depth and quality to your client relationships because it promotes a higher level of mental functioning both for you and your clients. In the development of high-quality level three relationships your ability to listen in the way we will be exploring is absolutely essential.

We live in a world where people increasingly get caught in the trap of feeling they need to go faster and attention spans are becoming shorter and shorter. The truth is that most of us are not aware of just how distracted we are.

Continuous partial attention

A condition that is deeply embedded in the way we now live is called 'continuous partial attention', a term coined by Linda Stone. The Wikipedia definition is 'The process of paying simultaneous attention to a number of sources of incoming information, but at a superficial level.'

It is easy to imagine in today's technology-driven world that if we feel distracted the problem lies in external sources of information. However, what we can often be unaware of is just how busy our own minds are. In our meetings we may think we are giving someone our full attention but be unaware of the amount of our own thinking that we are also paying attention to. For example, if you have ever felt that you were not really connecting with someone or were not fully present in a meeting then the cause of this will have been because of your own high level of mental activity.

So, before going any further let's look at a couple of examples that point towards the fact that there is another level of listening beyond what most people are used to.

In Nancy Kline's wonderful book *Time to Think: Listening to ignite the human mind* (2002) she cites the example of a survey where doctors were asked how long they listened to patients without interrupting them. The doctors said three minutes. The same doctors were then observed in consultation with their patients and the actual time they listened to their patients, without interruption, was 20 seconds.

Clearly, doctors and financial practitioners have different roles and it would be fair to say that doctors see a lot more people and are under more time pressure. However, what is clearly illustrated is that our perception of what is going on may not represent what is actually going on.

So, here is another example. At some of the workshops I run for financial practitioners participants do a thought awareness exercise. I ask everyone to find a partner and I carefully give the instructions twice and before beginning I ask for everyone's agreement that they have fully understood.

The exercise is very straightforward. One of the pair will talk and the other will listen, without interrupting, for five minutes. However, what happens, in pretty much every single case, is that the listening turns into a two-way conversation after about 30 seconds. It often surprises people, especially when they think they are good listeners, just how much thinking they have going on, how much they are applying their own judgements to what they are hearing, and how uncomfortable they are purely listening without responding. It is a useful exercise because it opens people up to the possibility of taking their ability to really listen to a whole new level.

You have to remember that all the time that you are doing the talking you are not finding out about your client. Clients don't come out of a meeting with you saying 'Wow, I'm so glad my adviser talks so much. I'm so impressed that they had so much to say because I now feel like we're really connected. I really feel I can trust this person!'

No, a client feels a deep connection to their adviser when they have been deeply listened to. The one thing that people truly value is to be listened to and feel understood. When you really invest in your client relationships by bringing this new level of listening to them, which we will come to shortly, you will be amazed at how this deepens the bond between you and your clients. This will improve the quality of the work you do together and also have other highly desirable by-products like being much more personally rewarding and creating more opportunity.

Let us consider the three kinds of listening.

Level one listening

This is where someone is listening but in such a way that they interrupt, finish sentences or when they are not doing either of those they are clearly waiting for a pause so that they can get their point across. So, in effect, they are not really listening at all.

I once had a client tell me that a potentially lucrative business partner had refused to do business with his company because one particular senior person at my client's company did not listen in meetings.

The feedback was that he interrupted, tapped his finger on the desk and, at times, actually came across as aggressive. It was also clear that this person's poor reputation had been passed on from one person to another and it was a humbling experience for my client to hear that this failure to listen had so far cost his company at least one lucrative relationship.

Usually, the underlying reason that people behave in this way is that they are feeling insecure. As a result they feel the need to try to exert control, push their own agenda and consequently fail to listen.

Another thing that can lead to poor listening is making assumptions. I have had several practitioners say to me that they know exactly what their clients want but before they have found out through deep listening. Believing you know what someone wants before you take the time to truly understand them will never be the basis of building a strong relationship or high-quality financial planning.

Level two listening

Level two listening is often mistaken for good listening. This is where, although the client is given space to talk and think, the listener is paying attention to the content. They are doing this so that they can solve, fix or give advice on what they are hearing. They may be making judgements about the client's circumstances, such as thinking about how they might structure the client's finances, for example. They are often looking for an opening so they can show the client how they can help or how knowledgeable they are.

This level is the most common way of listening in professional relationships because it seems to make sense. After all, if someone's professional training has taught him or her to offer solutions, consult or give advice then isn't this what they are supposed to do?

However, every time that we engage in our own thinking we are no longer with the client. We are up in our own head and, therefore, cannot possibly be getting a sense of where that person is really coming from in that moment. Most significantly, and this is right at the heart of building relationships, the feeling of connection will not develop.

This is not to say that there is not a time and place for delivering a plan and giving advice because there certainly is, but the tendency for practitioners is to make too many assumptions and jump in way too soon. Once again, what is often behind this is a feeling of insecurity, which drives a need to prove credibility.

It is a mistake to try to convince someone of your expertise. The very best way to prove your credibility is to demonstrate it by being willing to go deeper and really understand your client rather than trying to impress them with your knowledge.

Level three listening

Level three listening is listening with nothing on your mind. It is being genuinely interested in truly understanding someone, not at the level of content, but where they are coming from. This means completely holding a space for someone and allowing them to feel comfortable enough to really open up. It means dropping your concern about coming up with something, having an answer or thinking about how you are coming across. It means being vulnerable. Most people are not used to listening in this way and yet it is how to really deepen your client relationships.

When we really do listen completely openly, without pushing an agenda, without being judgemental and without being up in our own heads or oscillating between the client and what's in our own heads, it will create the relationship very differently.

The reason is because with this type of environment there is a depth of feeling that is reached that simply wouldn't happen at the two other levels. This is a space where people really connect because what you are doing is creating a safe environment where people feel at ease to share their innermost thoughts. If there is any hint of you being judgemental then this space will not be created.

Why this is just so important is because you want your client to have a clear mind. When people do their best thinking in your conversations the quality of the work you do will go up, often staggeringly.

Only level three listening will lead to creating level three relationships because it is truly client-centred listening. It deeply communicates the level of commitment that you, as the practitioner, are willing to bring to the relationship. The lower levels of listening, at best, will only result in transactional relationships.

Shifting to level three listening

I worked with a highly-qualified adviser who did business with his clients in a transactional way. The quality of the work, technically speaking, was excellent but his listening style was level two.

We talked about what it means to listen at level three and at a subsequent coaching session he shared with me his experience of a recent meeting with a couple who had been his clients for several years. Up to then his relationship with them had been focused only upon their finances. However, at their most recent meeting he listened with nothing on his mind, allowed a lot of space for his clients to think and was willing to ask more probing questions. He found that he was really impacted by what they were saying and he was both surprised and delighted at how the clients opened up to him. Subsequently, two things emerged from this experience that had not happened before.

Instead of simply discussing the investment of some money his clients shared how they wanted to live their lives in their forthcoming retirement years. He learnt more about them in that meeting than he had previously and because of his new understanding he was able to construct his advice in a way that connected directly with what really mattered to them. It was based upon the things they wanted to do and they engaged with possibilities to do things and live in a way that never would have happened without this new level of listening.

They had always wanted to take weekend breaks in various European cities but had never done so through being cautious with their money. Through listening and having his clients engage more deeply in what they wanted, the idea started to come alive for them. He was able to show them how it was possible to make these trips, which they began immediately, and still maintain the financial stability that was so important to them.

The second thing that happened was that they followed his advice to the letter and without question because they felt heard and understood. My client was deeply touched by the whole experience and he felt much more connected to his clients.

Aspects of level three

As level three listening is not what most people are used to doing I am including some key points that will help you shift your listening style into level three.

Even when listening with nothing on your mind you will have thoughts come into your mind. However, instead of holding on to the thoughts you can just notice them and then let them go. Even if you have some valid points come into your mind you can still let them go because if you keep paying attention to your thoughts then you won't be listening. Once the time comes for you to talk then you will know what to say, so you don't need to be concerned with hanging on to a thought you have whilst you are listening.

It is important to realise that when listening at level one or two your responses can easily be misaligned with what the client is really trying to communicate. At these lower levels of listening your attention would also be upon your own thinking and so you would miss what is really behind the words. With level three you are listening to understand, connect and be impacted rather than focusing upon the content.

You may feel that you don't have time to listen like this. However, if you really want to do outstanding work then there is no other way to listen. You will never experience the wonderful feeling of presence and connection that you get through deep level three listening by only listening at the lower levels. A concern that some advisers have expressed is that meetings will start taking far too long, but this just isn't the case. Initial meetings may be longer but, ultimately, they become more highly focused and may even be shorter because it is about quality not quantity.

Many advisers are very uncomfortable with silence within a conversation. In the example I gave of the listening exercise in the workshops one of the reasons that people give for jumping into the conversation is that they think they need to fill the void. This is a big mistake because you will often cut off your client's best thinking. When you create the space for someone the last thing you want to do is jump in because you feel uncomfortable. It is not about you and how you feel and wanting to jump in is just a sign that you've gone up inside your own head and have begun to feel insecure.

When you have nothing on your mind you will find that your own thinking will be more expansive. When our minds are quiet we automatically have more creativity, more internal freedom and the ability to respond with something relevant, useful and insightful.

Ultimately, the depth of the client relationships that you build will be defined by the quality of attention that you bring to them. When you give someone the gift of listening to them at level three what you communicate to your client is that what they think, feel and say really matters to you.

Thoughts to reflect on

There is another level of listening beyond what most people are used to.

Most of us do not even realise how distracted we are by our own thinking.

Your level of listening defines the depth of relationship that you create.

The highest quality of listening is deep level three listening with nothing on your mind.

Chapter 6

Effortless rapport

Chapter 6 – Effortless rapport

Rapport is like money: it increases in importance when you do not have it, and when you do have it, a lot of opportunities appear. **Genie Z. Laborde**

Creating deep rapport with your clients is essential to enable you to do high-quality work and just as with the quality of your listening, which we looked at in the previous chapter, there is a depth to the quality of rapport that you can create with someone that goes beyond what you might call social rapport.

With social rapport you can create an environment where you get along fine with someone and this level is perfectly adequate if you work at a transactional level. However, in order for your clients to really open up, think clearly and share what matters most to them, they need to feel safe, accepted and that they will not be judged. This requires a far deeper level of trust, rapport and connection between you.

Let us look at some of the reasons why it is so important to connect with your clients at a deeper level:

- Most people are not used to talking openly about what matters most to them in life and finances are often an uncomfortable subject for people. To overcome these barriers effectively people must feel comfortable enough in your presence to do so.

- It is crucial that your clients do their very best thinking in your meetings. From a clear mind people will often access a level of truth that has much more depth to it, which brings the process of financial planning to life and allows you to help them more effectively.

- When you are really present with people they will feel touched and from this your work together becomes far more meaningful.

- There are likely to be times when potentially delicate subjects need to be discussed. For example, this could be your client's mortality, differing life goals to their partner's or their fears about the future. With the appropriate level of rapport your clients will feel no need to hold back, be defensive or guarded in their responses.

- You need to be free to say what seems relevant without feeling the need to hold back. If you don't have sufficient rapport with someone then you may feel reluctant to be as candid as you could be or your communication may not be received in the way you would like it to be.

- If you do not agree with your client on something one sure way to lower the tone of the meeting is to openly disagree, which is basically making someone wrong. However, when you have deep rapport and they see that you are coming from a place of humility they will listen to you.

- We live in a time-poor world and while you never want to rush, you want to be efficient. When the tone of a meeting is high better results are often produced in less time.

Establishing deep rapport

At the very core of establishing deep rapport is your quality of mind. When your thinking is clear and you are present then you are fully available to the person you are with.

The reason that practitioners can often struggle to create deep rapport is that they have too much thinking going on. If you are up in your head thinking about what to say, what you think of the person, whether they might make a good client, how you are doing or how the meeting is going, then this will be a barrier to creating a strong human connection. You cannot be paying attention to your own thinking and be present at the same time.

How do you create deep rapport without thinking about doing it?

I was once a participant at a business training programme where we were being taught about establishing rapport and everyone was asked to move around the room for a few minutes trying to build rapport with people by using techniques, such as matching or mirroring or small talk. We were then stopped and asked to do the exercise again but this time by being fully present and connecting with each other on a more human level.

The difference was something we could all experience and the second way felt much less superficial. Instead of focusing upon doing something to build rapport, which takes mental work, rapport is simply a natural by-product of taking our attention off ourselves and relaxing. In fact, focusing on doing something is an obstacle to creating deep rapport. If we are in a clear and present state of mind then rapport will naturally take care of itself.

As you go into a meeting or conversation with your client you can simply reflect inwards just for a moment and ask yourself:

- Am I really here? Am I really present?
- Is my client with me or not?

If you find that you are still busy in your own mind or that your client appears this way then simply noticing will pull you back into the present and open up the potential for connection. As mentioned in the previous chapter on listening, one of the very best ways to have your mind clear is to listen at level three.

You may notice that during some meetings your feeling of rapport will lessen or even disappear. Our own and our client's state of mind will fluctuate because our thinking fluctuates. If you notice that you have started to focus upon your own thinking rather than your client then, once again, it is just the noticing that will pull you back to the present.

Having moods vs. moods having you

Something that is invisible to many people are their moods and it is important that you become more self-aware of your moods because sometimes we can get in our own way without realising it. This can be especially true when we interact with other people.

The fact is that all of us experience fluctuating moods, which are merely an indication of the fluctuations in the quality of our thinking. When our quality of thinking is low we will tend to feel insecure and our ability to connect meaningfully with other people will decrease. However, the problem is not the mood or feeling insecure; it is acting upon these kinds of feelings that can cause problems and affect our relationships negatively.

As an example, I once shared an office with a practitioner who was quite often in a low mood. Those times he was in a good mood he was charming and good at connecting with people. However, when in a low mood his manner would be curt, he would be control-ling in his behaviour and every now and then he would fall out with a client. In these low states of mind he would often be suspicious of clients' motives and think they were trying to get one over on him. Therefore, he would feel the need to be defensive, which was what led to the problems he experienced with people.

If we do not have an awareness of our moods it can be easy to succumb to them rather than being graceful and seeing them as merely indicators of our thought in the moment. Psychologist George Pransky (2013) in his insightful book *The Relationship Handbook* says 'People with destructive habits are feeling insecure'. With an awareness of why our moods fluctuate we can easily move through them when we are low and avoid behav-iours that can be anything from unproductive to totally undesirable.

George once shared with me an interesting story about a client he worked with. His client was an international chain of retail hairdressers and George was consulting for them on how to improve business performance.

One of the features of this business was that it had a 'redo' policy, so if any customer was unhappy with their haircut then the hairdresser would redo it free of charge. The company was interested in how this was working out and one of the things they did was to look at the correlation between the skill of the hairdresser and the amount of 'redo's. You would think that the less skilled the hairdresser the more likely a 'redo'.

What they found was that there was no correlation at all. The 'redo's were attributed to people all through the range of skill, right from the least experienced to the most expe-rienced. George showed the company that a 'redo' was most common when the stylist failed to create a good rapport with the client and they were not happy with how they were treated by the stylist.

What feeling insecure or being consumed with our own 'stuff' does is cause us to focus inwards and towards attending to our own needs. Often, the by-product of this is that the most important aspects of high-quality relationships, trust, authenticity and a feeling of connection, will be compromised because for these to develop our attention has to completely be on the other person.

So, if you are in a low mood and due to meet a client this does not need to be a problem if you have awareness of your internal state. When I occasionally find myself in this situ-ation it is a signal to me to completely direct my attention towards the person I am with. To make the point again, deep level three listening, which we covered in the previous chapter, is one of the very best ways to get present and have your thinking clear.

When people are suspicious

You are almost certainly going to experience times when someone is initially suspicious of you, perhaps at the first meeting with a potential client. This is entirely understandable because for some people this is a self-protection mechanism and you do not need to take it personally. You never need to start feeling insecure or anxious if someone seems to be holding back or is aloof. Gaining rapport is not dependent upon the other person initially engaging with you and the quickest way to help the other person's thinking settle is to keep your own mind clear.

I want to share an experience I had where someone who was initially suspicious of me became a very good client. This is not an illustration of a technique or something you should do; it is just an example of being present and what occurred to me in that moment.

I had received an introduction to Alan and he and I had exchanged emails and agreed to meet in person. So, we met up and began a conversation, but after about half an hour it felt to me that our discussion did not really have much depth and that we were going round in circles.

What occurred to me at the time was to say 'Can I say something please?' He said 'Yes' and I said 'You seem really uptight to me!'

At this point he sat back and said 'OK, I'll be honest. I'm suspicious of you and what you do because I've spoken with people like you before and I'm not sure if this is going to go anywhere.'

So, I reflected for a moment and what came to me was to say 'I can understand that you may feel that way, however, as we have only just met you don't know me or what I do and whatever you are thinking is based upon your own assumptions and not necessarily the truth. So, why don't we just hang out together for a while and have a real conversation instead? If nothing comes of it then that's fine, we have lost nothing other than a little time.' He agreed and because he relaxed and felt under no pressure we were able to have a much more meaningful communication.

Recounting this story, even for me, makes it seem as though I was being confrontational. However, it didn't come from me in that way and it was what occurred to me in the moment. We actually ended up having a great conversation and working together. We even looked back upon that first meeting and laughed about it.

Creating deep rapport is about quality of mind. When you are clear and present this is what allows your clients to have their minds settle and be present too. A deep bond is a natural by-product. Any form of working your agenda, employing a technique or a contrived way of building rapport will create the relationship very differently.

If you are in a meeting and have a sense that you have not yet built sufficient rapport then it would be pointless to proceed into anything further until it is sufficiently established. Exactly how you might do this will come from your own wisdom or insight in the moment because no two situations will ever be the same and, therefore, you cannot really plan for it other than to be fully present.

Thoughts to reflect on

Establishing deep rapport and connection with your clients is essential to enable you to do high-quality work.

Deep rapport allows your communication to be authentic, open and meaningful.

You create deep rapport through being present and fully focusing upon your client rather than by employing techniques.

Low moods never need to be a problem if we have self-awareness, understand why we have them and choose not to act from them.

If someone is initially guarded or aloof with you then staying in your clarity of mind is what keeps you connected to your wisdom and ability to build rapport and connection.

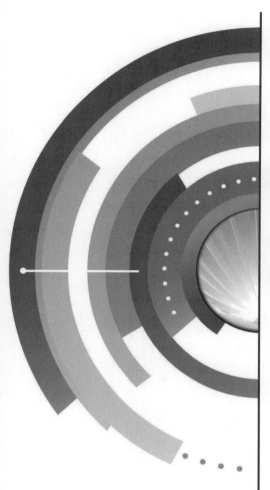

Chapter 7

The three levels of client conversation

Chapter 7 – The three levels of client conversation

In everyone's life, at some time, our inner fire goes out. It is then burst into flame by an encounter with another human being. We should all be thankful for those people who rekindle the inner spirit. **Albert Schweitzer**

The potential for your meetings is that your clients genuinely look forward to them and see them as an integral part of leading a higher quality of life, both in the future and right now. They can be the opportunity, possibly the only opportunity that people have to reflect and focus upon what really matters to them in life and how well aligned their finances are with their outcomes.

The real measure of the quality of your client conversations is not the content but the tone. It is the depth of feeling, degree of human connection and clarity of mind that contribute to making your client meetings of an exceptionally high quality. What people remember and value the most are powerful emotional experiences rather than intellectual discussions. So, a simple, yet very revealing indicator of the impact and quality of your client meetings is how invigorated, inspired and uplifted they are by them.

Take a moment to reflect on the following questions:

* Do you really know how engaging your clients find your meetings?
* Are you willing to take the risk of explicitly asking?

The reason that many people avoid engaging in conversations about finances, or feel apprehensive about them, is because doing so brings up a lot of insecure thinking, which causes them to feel bad. Therefore, it is absolutely essential that you have the presence and clarity of mind to guide your clients away from these kinds of state of mind and into healthier thinking. This is crucial to the process of really high-quality financial planning because you not only want to elicit meaningful objectives and outcomes from your clients, you also want them to gain real clarity and emotionally connect with their values.

It is feelings that matter

Have you ever stopped to consider what it is that you actually sell? I have asked many practitioners this question and, as you might imagine, you hear all sorts of different answers. Some say 'financial services', others say 'a secure future' and many say 'myself!' However, the practitioners who have the most powerful, positive impact with their clients understand that they are not just providing products or investments or solving financial problems; they know that clients will measure the value they get by how they feel. Feelings such as security, freedom, peace of mind, confidence and clarity are what make a real difference to people. Practitioners who miss this point make their job ten times more difficult because they are not focusing on what really matters to people which, ultimately, are feelings.

How people make decisions

A common misunderstanding is thinking that people make decisions logically. The fact is that people make decisions emotionally and they justify them with reason and logic. Exploring a question such as 'What do you want to do with the rest of your life?' with clients, when done in the right way, is an emotional as well as a practical exploration.

This is why conversations on a logical and analytical level are often not compelling for people because logic may make us think but it is emotion that makes us act. An analytical, numbers-based approach to financial planning might be fine back in your office but in client meetings it is highly likely to switch people off.

From your perspective, as the practitioner, going to a deeper emotional level with clients is highly rewarding because it becomes a much more meaningful experience for you too. It makes your work fun again. This results in better relationships because of the increased sense of connection between you and your client. In addition, when you facilitate your clients' reconnection with what matters most to them then they will see enormous value in their relationship with you. You are also highly likely to see a significant rise in referrals.

You no doubt experience a deeper connection with some of your clients because it tends to happen some of the time anyway. We all have people who we seem to naturally connect with in a deeper way, as if we are kindred spirits. However, it is both possible and important for you to create this high-quality environment as a standard way of operating. It will eventually become a deciding factor when you consider taking a client on in the first place because it is critical to the quality of work that you do.

Imagine that client conversations can potentially take place on three levels. It is so easy to miss out on connecting at a deeper level and so bypassing the real outcomes that people want, which can only be consistently reached through a level three relationship and level three listening.

Level one conversations

Level one conversations are those conversations that focus almost entirely on financial products, financial strategies, funds and investments. Of course, this is part of the financial planning process, so bringing them into the conversation is appropriate at the right time.

However, there seem to be many financial professionals who communicate almost entirely at this level and, sadly, both they and their clients are missing out on connecting with the ultimate outcomes. Therefore, a tremendous amount of value and opportunity is simply lost.

Communicating only at this level is like taxiing along the runway but never taking off because it is focusing upon the means to the end and not the end itself. Client conversations can be so much more than the purely transactional relationships found at this level and it is a long way from the potential of how you can really serve your clients. From a business viewpoint you are leaving a huge amount of untapped potential.

Keeping a conversation at level one does not create deeper, more insightful relationships. I'm not saying it doesn't happen but if it does, it is despite and not because of this level of conversation.

Giving out the wrong message

Many practitioners and firms want to operate at a deeper level with their clients, however, they give out the message that their primary function is providing products and investments.

The evidence for this is often in the output of marketing materials. For example, they have a website, literature and communications that explicitly promote products and focus upon financial issues. Many firms send out lengthy newsletters and briefs on products, investment returns or the latest financial 'in thing'. Some firms even go as far as having a live stock market feed on the homepage of the website.

This is what continues to make sense to a significant proportion of the profession but my expectation is that if there were some research done by those who produce such material, it would be discovered that there is very little interest from the majority of clients. Regular contact with your clients is good and I am not saying do not send timely, appropriate and useful information but you have to be aware of how you are directing someone's attention. If you keep pulling your clients' attention towards products, investments and financial issues then it is going to be that much more difficult to bring their attention to the bigger picture of what they really want from life.

How many people, do you think, really have a deep longing to own a pension plan, a bond, an annuity, a critical illness policy or to follow the markets?

Solely taking people's attention towards financial products and investments is exactly why many people avoid conversations about finances and find them dry and boring. In fact, the majority of problems that I have seen practitioners experience with clients, for example, challenges over fee levels, being questioned over the quality of the advice or losing clients almost always originate from the fact that the practitioner failed to engage the client emotionally and were only willing to stay on the perceived 'safe' ground of talking about what they themselves feel comfortable with.

The challenge for practitioners who have received their qualifications and permissions based largely upon their technical knowledge is understanding and acknowledging that most people are *not interested* at this level. Of course, people buy and own financial products but these are not what people ultimately want because they are the vehicle and not the destination.

If you give someone the choice between talking about themselves, their hopes, dreams, wants, needs and what matters most to them or having a conversation about pensions or what the markets are doing then what do you think they are going to choose?

Level two conversations

Many practitioners operate on the level of solving financial problems and so their focus of attention is upon identifying a client's problem to solve or a goal to accomplish. Clearly, to create a financial plan or strategy there has to be a beginning and an end point. Probably several end points. For example, retirement, death, school fees, life goals, sale of a business or maintaining a desired level of lifestyle. So, what makes sense to the practitioner is to elicit the problem or goal and then get to work on it.

Whilst it is extremely helpful to people to have their problems solved, if the focus of attention is solely upon identifying the problem and solving it then the deeper emotional engagement and opportunity to really understand the client is often bypassed. Regardless of the degree of sophistication of the problem or outcome, level two conversations lacking in emotional engagement result in transactional relationships (as do level one conversations) because what is at the centre is the problem or goal rather than the client.

The conversations you have with your clients can and should go deeper, if you want to make real impact. It is important for you to see the bigger picture and be willing to engage people emotionally, rather than just intellectually.

There are very sound business reasons for doing so. The standard of technical knowledge within the profession has gone up significantly and so a client going to any practitioner or firm will expect to get very high-quality advice. So, if you are working on the level of providing products and investments or solving a client's financial problems, even sophisticated ones, then from a client's perspective what makes you stand out? Any similarly qualified practitioner could do the same job.

The only real advantage you can create for yourself and your business is to create a powerful emotional experience for your client. The only way you can do this is to put the client at the very centre of everything that you do. What people are willing to pay the most for is a transformational experience. If you are instrumental in helping your clients identify what matters most of all, you inspire them to think, feel and act differently and stay with them to bring their desired outcomes into reality, then this creates exceptional value.

Level three conversations

Imagine your dream client for a moment. This is probably someone with whom you feel a real sense of human connection. They are willing to really open up and tell you everything. You feel you can speak candidly and openly with them, so that if you want to say something that challenges them it is accepted in the spirit it is given. They follow your advice and recommendations and trust you implicitly. They are an advocate and introduce you to other like-minded people. The relationship is one where you know you are really making a difference at a profound level.

Although this could happen through level one or level two conversations, it will be hit and miss because of the lack of emotional engagement. Effective, high-impact financial planning and advice must directly feed into what matters most to your clients, which is why it is essential that the conversation touches people emotionally.

A factor of modern existence is that many people are disconnected from what really matters to them in life. After all, how often do we sit down and deeply think about how we really want to live our lives and how aligned our finances are with this?

Therefore, it is up to you, as the professional, to create an environment where people feel comfortable enough to really open up. There is always the opportunity, and it is important that you take it, to explore what really matters to people and how they want to live their lives. Having a much deeper understanding of your client will influence the construction of your advice and recommendations because your thinking will be much more expansive. Let's look at an example.

The goal behind the goal

Imagine you have a business-owner client who tells you she wants to retire in ten years' time on a certain amount of income. Just knowing these hard facts tells you very little about the client and who she really is. The potential is there to have a conversation about what the client really wants to do with her time, how she wants to live and what this means to her. For example:

- What has she already thought of doing?
- What would she love to do?
- Why isn't she doing these things right now?
- Who are the most important people in her life and is there potential to do things for them or spend more time with them?
- What is most meaningful to her in life?
- How would she like to make a difference?
- What is she really passionate about?
- What will be her legacy?
- What are her fears, worries and concerns?

By exploring in this way you can often open up possibilities and take the quality and relevance of your work to a whole new level because you understand your client and what they want that much better.

When you create this kind of environment it leads to meetings that are insightful, inspiring, uplifting, enjoyable, creative and collaborative. A sure sign that your meetings are taking place at level three is that, as mentioned at the beginning of this chapter, your clients will feel invigorated, inspired and genuinely look forward to them.

What marks a level three conversation out is that it is a meaningful, emotional experience. The degree to which people will value their relationship with you and the whole financial planning process will come down to how meaningful it is to them. The problem with both level one and level two conversations is that they lack a deeper emotional engagement and, therefore, are purely transactional.

The real key to facilitating level three conversations is your intention and how you show up to the conversation. Conversations stay at level one and level two because the practitioner only wants them to be at this level. I would also add that some practitioners seem to think they are having level three conversations when, in fact, they are having level one or two conversations. My experience is that only a small percentage of practitioners actually have deep, level three client conversations.

At level three the practitioner will also eventually advise on products and investments and provide solutions, just as at levels one and two. However, their primary intention is firstly to understand the client. It is to get a real sense of who the person is, what really matters to them and how they want to live their lives. This is what moves relationships away from being transactional and significantly increases the degree of trust. Importantly, it is what really starts to differentiate you. A client could have a level one or level two conversation with any practitioner, but very few are willing to operate at level three.

To make it crystal clear what makes a level three conversation different from levels one and two is that they will always have the following elements:

- Your primary intention is to clearly understand and connect with the client.
- You establish deep rapport.
- You listen at level three.
- You are willing to explore the deeper meaning behind the client's goals and objectives.
- You ask appropriate, high-quality questions (which we will come to in the next chapter).
- You are willing to keep probing until you know that you have got to the core. It is a co-discovery process because people often have hidden goals that only emerge within a powerful conversation.

Setting the tone

It is your responsibility to set the tone and direction of your client conversations. As I am sure you already know, clients will often come to you and ask for products and investments or to have a financial problem solved. So, this is a conversational fork in the road. You can stay at level one or two or you can direct the client into level three.

What is most important in redirecting your client towards a deeper conversation is your quality of mind. When it makes complete sense to you to have level three conversations and you feel entirely secure about it, then redirecting the client will be natural and easy. If you feel insecure it is much more difficult because the client will sense that something is amiss.

Here's an example of how you could redirect someone into a deeper conversation:

Mr/Mrs/Miss Client, my job is to help you accomplish the goals, objectives and outcomes that are most important to you. As I am sure you can appreciate, money is the means to an end and not the end itself. It is what the money can do for us or what we can do with the money that ultimately matters. Are you happy for me to ask you some questions and get a better understanding of what you really want to accomplish?

You can also begin to set the tone even before you meet by letting the client know what is required (meetings do not have to be in person, more and more advisers are using Skype or similar applications).

Something I have done for several years as a coach is to send people two questions that I want them to consider before our initial meeting. I send these by email and ask them to send me their answers before we meet or have them ready for our meeting. Examples of the types of question I use (courtesy of Rich Litvin) are as follows:

- If this turns out to be the most powerful conversation you have all year – how will you know? I.e. what would you see, hear and feel during or immediately after our conversation or in the days, weeks and months ahead?
- Where are you most likely to get stuck or stop yourself from succeeding? In other words, if you wind up being disappointed with your results, why will that be? The point of this question is that you already know, in advance, exactly why you are going to fail at some endeavour... so it's very powerful to write that reason down before you begin. That way, we can eliminate that reason now and take clear action to create the results you want.

This really helps to focus people's minds before we meet. I have had many people comment that receiving these questions made them realise that we were going to have much more than a 'chat' and that the conversation was going to be important.

From my perspective I also want to test the person's willingness to do the task. My experience is that almost everyone will engage with the questions and, often, I have had people send me lengthy answers that they have clearly put a lot of thought into. If they did not answer the questions I would want to know why and, as it has done in the past, it would cause me to question whether I would want to engage them as a client.

These questions can easily be adapted for your purposes (examples below) or you can make up your own. If you are concerned about the reaction of potential clients when receiving these kinds of question, then don't be. They will work for you rather than against you because they demonstrate that you are putting the client right at the centre from the very beginning.

- What would you most like to get from our meeting and how will you know if it has been a highly productive use of your time? I.e. what would you see, hear and feel during or immediately after our conversation or in the days, weeks and months ahead?
- What are your most important outcomes and goals in life that require planning?
- What areas of concern do you have with your finances, both short term and long term?
- What would give you peace of mind once you know you have things in hand?

All client conversations can be at level three

Clearly, you can have several different types of conversations with your clients depending upon which stage of the relationship you are at. For example, you may have clients who you have known for many years and you meet to review their circumstances and arrangements. Whichever stage you are at, the potential is for all your conversations to have the qualities of a level three conversation, even though the focus and content may differ. You can bring a clear and present mind, create deep rapport and listen at level three within all your interactions.

Thoughts to reflect on

The potential for your meetings is that clients find them inspiring, invigorating and uplifting.

Your client's depth of emotional engagement determines their perception of value. The lower the emotional engagement, the lower the perception of value.

Level three, emotionally engaging, conversations are the foundation for creating exceptionally high value for your clients.

People make decisions emotionally and justify them with reason and logic.

You set the tone and direction of your client conversations and it is up to you to facilitate a richer, deeper emotional experience for your clients.

Chapter 8

The art of client-centred questioning

Chapter 8 – The art of client-centred questioning

Successful people ask better questions, and as a result, they get better answers.
Tony Robbins

All the practitioners I know who have mastered the art of deep client engagement are outstanding at the discovery phase. They put a great deal in at this stage because they understand that getting to their clients' core values, eliciting meaningful goals, objectives and outcomes and getting commitment are all essential to the level of engagement in the relationships and the quality of the work.

Exploring what your clients want from life will often be a co-discovery process because many people have hidden goals and dreams in life. Genie Z. Laborde (1995), wrote in her book *Influencing with Integrity: Management skills for communication and negotiation*, 'Most people do not know what their most valued outcome is. As you probe for their outcomes, new ones often pop up – ones they did not even know they wanted, outcomes so deeply buried in their unconscious minds that they were unaware of their desires.'

If you are going deep enough then, in many cases, your clients will have fresh thinking, insights and realisations that they may not have previously had or, at least, had given little thought to. Therefore, you have the opportunity to create a conversation of real substance and the process of connecting and reconnecting people to what really matters to them has enormous value.

Often, financial services firms are explicit about the 'financial planning process', which is presented as a number of steps with the first or second step being about 'identifying needs, goals and objectives'. However, the way this step is approached can easily lack depth and fail to engage people emotionally if the conversation is treated as a logical, left-brained exercise. It is your willingness to hold the intention of deeply understanding your clients that facilitates a powerful discovery phase and sets the tone for the whole relationship.

In the previous chapters we have looked at why the client relationship must be based on giving, level three listening, building deep rapport and level three conversations. The questions that you ask your clients are also of paramount importance because these will direct the focus of their thinking. Questions can perform many functions and just some of them are:

- Focusing attention
- Eliciting information
- Exploring purpose, meaning and value
- Stimulating thinking
- Opening up choices

- Increasing awareness
- Challenging assumptions

Your questions will demonstrate the degree of curiosity, caring and confidence that you bring to the process of discovery. These, along with deep level three listening, are what elicit very high-quality information.

The three approaches to discovery

There are three approaches you can take to having powerful discovery conversations that help to connect people to their best thinking:

1. A scripted conversation
2. A free-flowing conversation
3. A combination of scripted conversation and free-flowing conversation

A scripted conversation

There are several proprietary brands of scripted client conversations that are available to financial practitioners and what these do is give you a track to run on. Several years ago, along with financial planner, Andy Jervis (see Chapter 13 for Andy's contribution) I created a client conversation called 'Client Magic', which is reproduced at the end of this chapter.

The best of these proprietary conversations, although all different in the way they are structured and the questions they use, all have the potential to do the same thing when used effectively. They facilitate level three conversations by helping you to set the right tone, create emotional engagement, have clients do their best thinking and elicit high-quality information.

However, the power is not in the questions alone; it is in the quality of mind that you bring to the process. Unless clients feel completely comfortable and reassured when talking to you the answers they give to your searching questions may be what they think you want to hear rather than the deeper truth.

What will also lower the quality tone of a conversation is you going up into your head and trying to remember the questions or think about what you are doing. Clearly, there is a learning curve to any kind of process, so having the questions in front of you is fine and certainly preferable to getting caught up in your thinking about what to ask. The more experience you gain the smoother and more flowing the process becomes but there is absolutely no reason why you cannot make it highly effective right from the very beginning, even with very little practice.

A free-flowing conversation

A free-flowing conversation is one where there is no specific script but this does not mean that the conversation has no direction or is any less powerful than a scripted conversation. In fact, free-flowing conversations have the potential to be the most powerful of all because, rather than following a process, you can intuitively respond to your client, which will often take the conversation to an even deeper and more insightful level.

As a guide there are four basic categories of question that you can ask. Remember that the discovery process is not just for your benefit; it is just as much a discovery for your clients too:

1.   Situation – Where are you now?

2.   Objectives and outcomes – Where are you going?

3.   Meaning – What is the deeper meaning, value and purpose of your objectives and outcomes?

4.   Obstacles – What could stop you?

Let's explore each category in a little more detail.

Situation – Where are you now?

The basic tool for gathering information is some kind of fact find but as a tool to get a sense of who the person is and where they are coming from it is of very little help. All a traditional fact find will do is provide you with a snap shot in time of hard data. Of course, this is essential information but it tells you very little in terms of the story behind the snap shot in time. For example:

•   Who is this person?

•   Where are they coming from?

•   How did they get to where they are now?

•   Is their financial situation improving or declining?

•   Why did they make the decisions they have already made?

•   Are these decisions still relevant today?

•   What is their attitude to money?

•   What kind of relationship do they have with money?

•   What are their fears, worries and concerns?

Specific questions that will elicit this kind of information are:

•   Tell me about you?

•   Tell me about your business?

•   How would you describe your relationship with money?

•   What is your current financial reality, as you see it?

•   Why did you take out your current arrangements?

•   What is your biggest financial problem?

•   What keeps you awake at night?

•   What would you most like to change/have be different?

•   What are your current priorities?

•   How do you see the future?

- Is there anything else you would like me to know?
- Is there anything you do not want me to know?

Every single person and situation will be different and with practice and experience it will occur to you which line of questioning will be appropriate for each one. When you create the right kind of environment most people enjoy opening up and talking about themselves. This in turn creates a great deal of value for the client because the dynamic of being asked questions and being listened to is entirely different to them trying to think things through on their own.

You do not need to be concerned with getting it 'right' because there is no one right way. Your quality of mind and intention are far more important than any particular question you can ask. If you concern yourself too much with having to get it 'right' then this will simply make you feel unnecessarily insecure and will lower the quality of the conversation.

Objectives and outcomes – Where are you going?

You must be willing to really dig deep with people. This is not being intrusive; it is being professional. When you are coming from a place of service and with your client right at the centre then it makes complete sense to ask people to think about what really matters to them.

Ultimately, for planning purposes, you will want to agree specific, measurable objectives because from these a clear plan of action can be created. For example, if you are helping someone plan for retirement then the amount of money they want, when they want it by and all the logistical details are important. However, before you get to this level of detail you want to explore the bigger picture and create the emotional engagement.

Questions that elicit and clarify goals, objectives and outcomes are:

- What will make this meeting a brilliant use of your time?
- What do you want to accomplish in life – what would you do if it really were entirely up to you?
- What do you want to do with the rest of your life?
- What is your dream?
- How do you really want to see your future?
- What are your objectives/financial objectives?
- What do you want your legacy to be?
- What does this goal (outcome) look like specifically?
- How will you know when you have it? What will you see, hear and feel that lets you know?
- When do you want to have this by? What is your time frame on this?
- What is the order of priority of your goals?
- Do you think we now have a clear picture and understanding of what you want to accomplish?

A concern that some practitioners express is that, if they have a more open level three conversation with their client rather than one at level one or two, the conversation could easily stray completely off track and become irrelevant or diluted.

Sometimes people do wander off somewhere irrelevant or unproductive within a conversation and, as a coach, I have experienced this at times with my own clients. The way to deal with this is to be present enough to notice that this is happening and then to bring it back to the matter in hand. At times I have framed this with a client by saying beforehand that, whilst the intention is not to cut them off, if the conversation does stray I will interrupt and bring it back on track and check that they are OK with this.

Meaning – What is the deeper meaning, value and purpose of your objectives and outcomes?

As we saw in the previous chapter, people do not make decisions based purely on logic; they base them upon emotions and then justify their decisions with reason and logic. Getting to the deeper meaning is where the real power in a conversation lies because it engages someone emotionally and puts them in touch with their values.

For example, imagine your client said 'I'd like to make provision for my two children to be able to go to university and not leave with a ton of debt.'

This could be a level two conversation at this point if you dive straight into the logistics (how much money required, by when). However, you can facilitate a much richer level three experience for your client. The purpose of doing this is that it creates clarity of mind, helps enormously in the decision-making process and with the ongoing commitment to a particular goal. So, by simply asking some further questions and listening at level three, you can improve the quality of your meetings and the experience of your client considerably.

To reiterate the point again, if you want to explore something more deeply with a client then it is respectful and important to ask permission to do so first, so you might simply ask, 'May I ask you a couple more questions about this?' Once you have permission to proceed then the ground for asking is that much more fertile.

You: 'So, if you were able to fund your children through university and not leave with a ton of debt, what would it mean to you to be able to do this?'

Client: 'It would mean a great deal. I want them to be able to enjoy life and not struggle like I did.'

You: 'Just imagine we were here several years from now looking back, what would it mean to you having funded your kids through university and seen them leave without a ton of debt?'

Client: 'I would feel a great sense of accomplishment and satisfaction. It would be wonderful.'

You: 'And what makes this important to you and for you?'

Client: 'I love my children and I want to do what I can for them. It's what I've worked towards all these years. It gives me a sense of inner peace.'

When you ask questions that elicit meaning the person you are talking to really experiences those emotions in the here and now. You can think of these states as the goal behind the goal. On the surface there is the external outcome, in this case we are talking about making provision for the children to go to university, and there are the internal values, which in this case are feelings of accomplishment and satisfaction, wanting them to be able to enjoy life and not struggle and a sense of inner peace.

For any and every decision we make there are these emotional values. Although they can seem more nebulous they are extremely important. You cannot guess them and you cannot skip them if you want to do work of the highest quality and engage your clients deeply in the process of financial planning. If you dive into the logistics of something without exploring the meaning it just becomes a transaction.

Questions that elicit meaning:

- What would it mean to you now looking forward to accomplishing this/your goals?
- Going out into the future now looking back, what would it mean to you having already accomplished these goals?
- What's important to you about...?
- What would it mean to...?
- On a scale of one to ten, how important is this to you right now?
- What would having/accomplishing ... ultimately do for you?
- For what purpose?

When you are willing to explore the meaning it connects things for people at higher, more abstract levels and they think more about the 'big picture'. It creates emotional engagement and it helps people make better, clearer decisions.

Obstacles – What could stop you?

It is not just eliciting what your clients want that is important; you also want to explore what they think could stop them or what gets in the way of what they want. The financial services business places a lot of importance upon creating cover for life's unforeseen circumstances and, of course, it is wise counsel to ensure that your clients become financially bullet proof in this way.

However, the obstacles that you see and the ones that your clients see might be two totally different things and having the conversation about what your clients see as potential obstacles could be quite enlightening, both for them and you. Once again, the more relevant the information you base your plan on the more compelling and appropriate it is for your client.

Questions that elicit potential obstacles:

- What obstacles might there be?

- What could stop you?
- What do you see as the risks?
- What concerns do you have?
- What could get in the way?
- What do you want to avoid?

Terry's story

Terry shared a story about a situation he had with one of his existing clients, Lisa, who had a significant amount of money sitting on deposit.

Prior to having deeper conversations with his clients Terry's conversations had always centred on the money and the products. He knew that Lisa had been sitting on this money for some time and he had raised the issue of making it work harder on a couple of previous occasions but his suggestions had fallen on deaf ears, which frustrated him.

At a coaching session we talked about this and where his frustration was coming from. I asked him whether it was coming from the client sitting on the money or his thinking about his client sitting on the money. We also talked about how his client didn't seem to want to open up to him. Upon reflection, Terry could see how he had been getting caught up in his thinking about the situation, which is something that we all do from time to time.

When Terry next spoke to Lisa they had a much more open conversation. With his genuinely curious and open state of mind he noticed how she was much more willing to open up to him and she shared that she wanted to leave her position as marketing director of a large company and set up her own consultancy. She had been reluctant to commit the money to an investment because she might need it to support herself through the transition.

Terry realised, through having this deeper conversation, that focusing on where to put the money right now was not useful or appropriate. It was far more helpful to Lisa to be able to articulate her issue and share it without feeling she needed to hold back. They talked about this exciting new project and what it meant to her and she was deeply grateful to Terry for listening and helping her get more clarity.

As a result of being willing to ask questions, really listen and pick up on what he was experiencing the bond between them deepened because it was all about the client. Terry helped Lisa through this period of her life and she went on to create a successful business of her own. Ultimately, he did good business and he was also referred on to some other family members because of the bond and degree of trust he had built.

A combination of scripted conversation and free-flowing conversation

This is exactly as it says. You might have a track to run on but are also prepared to come off that track and go with what makes sense at the time. This can sometimes be the entirely right thing to do because there is no system that is going to fit every situation all of the time.

If you look at the 'Client Magic' conversation you will see that it is a scripted conversation. However, there will be occasions where changing the flow, order or line of questioning is appropriate and exactly the right thing to do. For example, you may have occasions when you want to explore a particular response from your client in more detail because you sense that it is a highly significant issue or concern for them.

In your client meetings nothing is more important than being present and responding to what is going on. If you are too committed to a process then there will be times when it lowers the tone of the meeting rather than making it more effective because it has become about the process rather than putting the client first.

Ultimately, the whole basis for high-impact financial planning is the quality and depth of your up-front discovery phase. The higher the quality of the information that you elicit the better the job you can do for your clients and the more meaningful and relevant it becomes for them.

Thoughts to reflect on

The discovery phase must be emotionally engaging to have real impact.

Your questions demonstrate the degree of curiosity, caring and confidence you bring to the process of discovery.

There are four basic categories of questions – situation questions, objective and outcome questions, meaning questions and obstacle questions.

Ultimately, it is your quality of mind that brings the discovery phase to life.

The higher the quality of the information that you elicit the better the job you can do for your clients and the more meaningful and relevant your work becomes for them.

Client Magic – client questionnaire

Mr/Mrs/Ms Client, My job is to help you accomplish the goals, objectives and outcomes that are most important to you. As I am sure you can appreciate, money is the means to an end and not the end itself. It is what the money can do for us or what we can do with the money that ultimately matters. Are you happy for me to ask you some questions and get a better understanding of what you really want to accomplish?

Part 1

1. What do you want to accomplish in life – what would you do if it really were up to you?

And what else?

Summarise and repeat back the answers before asking questions 2, 3 and 4.

2. What would it mean to you now looking forward to accomplishing your goals?
3. Going out into the future now… looking back what would it mean to you having already accomplished your goals?
4. What makes all this important to you?

Having got a sense of the broader perspective it is important that we create measurable and specific goals so that we can create a clear action plan

Goal	Date to achieve	Amount (£)	Client's priority

Goal	Date to achieve	Amount (£)	Client's priority

Part 2

Read back the specific goals to your client so they hear you say them and ask:

1. Do you think we now have a clear picture and understanding of what you want to accomplish?
2. As you consider your goals and what it means to accomplish them, what makes all this worth doing?
3. How does all of this enrich your life?

Chapter 9

Perfect delivery – every time

Chapter 9 – Perfect delivery – every time

The single biggest problem in communication is the illusion that it has taken place.
George Bernard Shaw

The time will come when you have gathered enough information from your clients to construct a plan and you agree to meet again to deliver and discuss your recommendations. As with every conversation that you have, what determines the quality of the communication is not simply the content but the experience your client has. Level three conversations are the benchmark of all your client interactions and not just in the discovery phase.

In the meetings when you are primarily gathering information your clients should have been doing most of the talking. This time around you are going to have greater input because you will be sharing your plan and ideas and it is essential that you keep your clients engaged and avoid them switching off.

Before you meet it is wise to check with your client to see if anything has changed since your last meeting (something it's sensible to do at every client meeting) and before delivering your plan. If you are going deep enough in your discovery meetings then this can have the effect of stirring things up and it could be that your client has insights, realisations and further private discussion about what they want or do not want from life. You want to avoid being caught out having created a masterpiece of a plan only to be told that circumstances have changed. So, you may wish to do this prior to your meeting by email or telephone call.

It is also important to ensure that the people who need to be involved will be at the meeting. If, for example, you are dealing with a couple then you will want them both there. The last thing you want is to enter the meeting, be told that one of them could not be present and that the information will be passed on, because it could easily be miscommunicated.

The meeting

Imagine coming out of a client meeting where you presented your plan and recommendations and feeling it was one of the best, if not the very best, meeting, that you ever had.

How would you know?

While we could describe the positive outcomes of a meeting in many ways, what defines great communication is the feeling of heartfelt connection between people. It is warm feelings of goodwill, connection, openness, understanding and trust that we remember just as much as the result.

Your clarity of mind is your greatest asset because when you are clear and present you will be sensitive to what is going on with your client and in the environment. You will no doubt have prepared well and thoroughly for your delivery meeting but it is a mistake to go in with a rigid idea about how you want to present your plan. Life is happening moment by moment and you can never fully account for the dynamic of the meeting beforehand.

By being highly conscious of your client's degree of engagement you can adjust your communication accordingly by allowing your wisdom to guide you.

Anna's story

Anna, a financial planner, shared her experience of a recent client meeting. She would always prepare thoroughly for a presentation meeting and she would also have a very rigid game plan of how she wanted the meeting to go, having tried to think of and take into account every possible eventuality. If she ever conducted a meeting and it began to go differently to how she wanted it to, she could find herself losing concentration and feeling unsettled, which could negatively affect the degree of rapport she had with her client.

She shared that on the way to this particular meeting she noticed how she was revving up her mind with a lot of thinking and it occurred to her how this might negatively affect the meeting with her client. So, although she was prepared, as always, this time she allowed herself to go in with a quiet mind and let her intuition guide her. She said that afterwards, as she drove back to her office, she had a smile on her face because it had been such an inspiring meeting and she felt a real sense of connection with her client. She had delivered what she wanted to and yet she had also been highly responsive to her client because she wasn't trying to control every step of the situation, which is what she had been doing before.

Opening your meeting

While there are no hard and fast rules about how you set up a meeting at the beginning, at all times it is about putting your client right at the centre and so it is important to gain permission to proceed and ensure that they feel comfortable and know what to expect.

You may wish to agree the timeframe for the meeting because doing so will focus your and your client's attention. At times there may be a lot to get through but nevertheless an hour is about how long most people can pay attention before needing a break.

Your degree of presence is what allows you to be aware of what is going on with a client and if you see them switching off then continuing will be counterproductive. If you agree a time limit or a set time to finish it gives you licence to bring a meeting back on track if you find it being sidetracked into irrelevancy. If you feel that the energy really has gone from a meeting then your best option may be to bring it to a close and set a time to meet again.

Building bridges

It can be highly beneficial to link the past to the present in your meetings because without linking what has gone on before to what is happening now there is a danger that in each of your meetings with a client you will be starting all over again each time, which is something you want to avoid because of the time it takes to reconnect.

If you ever watch a documentary on a television channel that has advertisement breaks you will notice that after each break the first thing that happens is a quick recap of where things left off and what is going on. This is because they understand the importance of quickly re-engaging people.

So, you can simply summarise in a few sentences what has gone on before, which will re-engage the client. As an example:

> *Mr/Mrs/Miss Client, last time we met we spent some time clarifying your most important goals and what it means to accomplish them. Your immediate priorities are making provision for... and this is important to you because you want to experience peace of mind and make a difference.*

What you are doing here is backtracking to what went on before and repeating three or four facts about your previous meeting or other relevant details. You must be careful to use only indisputable factual information. What you will usually find is that you will see your client agreeing with you as they check with themselves the validity of what you are saying. If you say something that is not true or that they may not agree with then you will quite likely lose rapport instead of building it quickly.

It is important to pay attention to key words, phrases and expressions that your clients use to articulate their personal values because these are the keys to their emotions. For example, if your client has told you they want to experience 'peace of mind' and 'make a difference' then use these phrases back to them because this is what is important to your client. If you use different words or change the phrase you will lose the impact.

It is a good idea to note down these key words, expressions and phrases that each of your clients use when expressing their values. You can then refer back to them and use them in your next communication, which is very powerful because you are then really talking to them in their language.

Relating to the meaning

People take action because of the depth of meaning of something and a simple rule is 'no meaning, no action', which is why it is so important to elicit meaningful outcomes in the discovery phase. When your recommendations align perfectly with your client's goals, objectives and outcomes it is proof that you were really listening. People feel inspired when they are living in accordance with their highest values and, therefore, when your plan specifically and clearly feeds into these you are almost guaranteed a high level of client engagement.

As you present your solutions it is important that your clients make the connection, in their minds, between the outcome, the meaning and the required action. When there is a clear link between what they want and what you are recommending then there is no basis for resistance. On the other hand people will be reluctant to do something that does not make sense to them.

Switching people off with too much information

The financial services industry should hold its head in shame over the amount and complexity of information it expects people to digest. You need to be aware that it can be very easy to disengage people if you introduce too much complexity. I will share two examples with you of how people can switch off.

A practitioner I know shared with me that due to him not having authorisation to give advice on a certain complex tax situation with a client he asked a colleague who was authorised to accompany him. So, they went to see the client and the meeting was a disaster. He told me that the adviser who accompanied him talked nothing but technical speak for over an hour and he could see the client's eyes becoming more and more glazed over. The client ended up completely disengaged.

Another example concerns the length of the plan you create. Longer is not better! My company used to coach clients through a system called the One Page Business Plan, which was exactly as it says. Even the business plan for a large company had to be on one page of A4, with a limited number of characters, because that was the whole point. Clients loved the simplicity because of the clarity they got.

Less is more

A business consultant I know had a business that helped doctors to run more efficient practices. Their process was that they would go into the practice and do an in-depth analysis of how the practice was operating. They would then create a long, detailed report and recommendations and go back to present this to the doctors and staff.

What the consultant could not understand was why they got so much pushback on the reports. There would be lots of questions, objections and failure to follow the recommendations even though the analysis was accurate and the recommendations completely valid.

What changed the situation was when the consultant learned about state of mind and what creates it because she now understood that the sheer amount of information was making some people feel intimidated and uneasy. When people start to get up in their heads and do too much thinking it will lower the tone of a meeting and potentially cause all sorts of unnecessary problems.

Once she realised what was happening she reduced the reports to a simple one pager with just one or two recommendations. Immediately, the client's level of engagement went up and she experienced no more problems because the feeling in the meetings remained uplifting and inspiring rather than causing people to resist and be defensive.

Different people will have different capacity for the amount of information that they are comfortable with handling and processing, so it is important to pay attention to the client's state of mind and make adjustments as you go along, if necessary.

If you have a lot of information to deliver then you will be far better off delivering it in smaller chunks, rather than just doing an information dump. For example, you can deliver one chunk and then check in with your clients by asking a question such as 'Does this make sense, so far?' or 'Do you have any comments or questions?' By gaining agreement at each stage you can keep things moving forward whilst keeping your client engaged.

Talk from your experience

What makes presentations dry and boring for clients is if you talk from your intellectual mind to their intellectual mind. As we saw in Chapter 1, from a client's perspective financial planning is not an analytical, hard fact, number-crunching, linear and technical process, so you want people's thinking to be expansive, rich and engaged.

You can bring information alive through stories and sharing your own personal experience. What this does is have people use their imaginations, create meaning and more easily grasp concepts.

When you reflect you can find many stories from everyday life that you can use to make a point. You also can share your own plan, why you chose to do certain things and why it makes sense to you. You do not have to give people the figures or personal information but it is very reassuring for people to know that you take your financial planning seriously and that you have faced similar problems, issues and challenges.

Take care of your own level of engagement

The most important thing in your presentation meetings, at all times, is your client's level of engagement. The only way you can successfully facilitate your client's high engagement is by taking care of your own level of engagement. If you are attached to the outcome, doing too much thinking, talking at someone, or needing to be seen as the expert all the time, then you will begin to lose the warm feeling connection.

At times, every single one of us will experience our minds wandering in client meetings. It is having the awareness that this is happening that is crucial because as soon as you know then you can redirect your attention back to the present.

Thoughts to reflect on

The most important aspect of presenting your plan is your client's level of engagement.

Your clarity of mind is what allows you to facilitate high-quality presentation meetings.

A successful meeting is a balance between being thoroughly prepared and being responsive to your clients and the environment in the moment.

Deliver information in manageable chunks, bring it alive through stories and your own experience and clearly relate your recommendations to your client's goals, outcomes and values.

Chapter 10

The adviser as a coach

Chapter 10 – The adviser as a coach

Usually the brain that contains the problem also contains the solution – often the best one. **Nancy Kline**

Genuine financial planning, where your client is right at the centre, is more than just making the numbers work. That is the outer game but what about the inner game? If your goal, as the practitioner, is to genuinely help your clients accomplish what is most important to them and help them to lead a better quality of life then, at times, you may need to coach them.

Many people's thinking in the area of money is not good. They may feel insecure about money, they may worry about it or be preoccupied about it. Many people have poor habits with money. They may overspend, save little and have made poor choices. Often, family breakdown can be attributed to insecure thinking about money. Clearly, all of these things will detract from someone's quality of life.

If someone's financial adviser isn't going to help them have a healthy relationship with money, then who is? The answer is probably nobody.

The future of financial advice: the holistic approach

The practitioners who will lead the way in financial services will be those who help their clients have a healthy relationship with money because it is such a crucial factor in leading an authentic and meaningful life.

Simply providing products or solving specific financial issues does not directly address someone's relationship with money. Historically, financial advisers (with exceptions) have avoided coaching, teaching and educating their clients about how to have a healthy relationship with money, primarily because the business has been so transaction focused.

However, the commercial value in purely transactional relationships is decreasing rather than increasing. As we saw in Chapter 1, the highest value in the client-centred relationship is in the conversations that take place between the practitioner and the client. This is the area with the most upside potential for making a difference and also an area with significant revenue potential for your business.

In many ways, the capabilities of the client-centred adviser are akin to those of a coach; building deep rapport, deep listening and client-centred questioning are the foundation of both effective coaching and financial planning. We will shortly explore where coaching a client may be applicable but before we do this it is important to understand the distinction between coaching and advising.

Coaching vs. advising

With advice you are very clearly suggesting the action that your client takes to fulfil a predetermined outcome. The reason that advice is being provided is because the client has little or no knowledge in the area of advice being given. For example, if you are advising them on the details of a suitable financial strategy to accomplish a goal then this is your domain.

Coaching, like financial planning, is outcome based but when coaching someone you are not advising, consulting, counselling or mentoring them. Instead you are helping someone raise their awareness, create greater choice and better utilise their innate ability to accomplish what is important to them. There can be an element of teaching within coaching and the purpose of this is to facilitate and support new thinking and behaviour within the client.

No agenda

One of the most important things I have learned from being a coach is that you may well be the only person in someone's life who has no hidden agenda. Many times my clients have told me that one of the biggest values they get from the work we do together is that I tell them how I see a situation. I may not always be right, but that's fine because I have their permission to say what I see.

The truly client-centred adviser is never following their own agenda; they are purely focused upon helping their clients get what they really want. They are not holding back through fear of a negative reaction, looking foolish or because they are worried about how they are coming across.

Right at the very core of this is the state-of-mind factor because it is only from a high level of psychological functioning that we have the quality of our own thinking that can positively impact the client.

What makes a great coach is not the person who has the best coaching model or the most tools in his or her toolbox. It is someone who has a very high degree of mental clarity because, as we saw in Chapter 3, 'Being is the new doing', what really impacts people is who you are being, far more than what you are doing.

What is a coaching situation?

There could be an almost infinite number of specific situations where someone would benefit from coaching but let us consider four that relate to financial planning and the accomplishment of your client's goals.

1.   As we have already seen in previous chapters, skilfully eliciting your client's most important goals, objectives and outcomes is often a form of coaching. Many people have not really thought very deeply about what they want from life. For instance, if you were to ask your client 'What is most important to you in life?', then exploring this effectively is going to be deeply influenced by your state of mind, your willingness to listen at level three and to keep probing until you get to meaningful answers.

2.   There are going to be times when your client lacks the resources to accomplish their desired goals and this is a classic situation where you coach a client through the situation because there are many potential outcomes. They may decide to choose a

different goal, they may reduce the size of a goal or they may choose to raise their game to meet the goal. Telling, suggesting or influencing them as to what you think is not your job, unless you are specifically asked for an opinion. Instead you coach them to realise their own solution.

3. Even when the client has clear goals, objectives and outcomes they can easily, and most likely will at some point, come off track, which can result in the goal getting pushed further into the future rather than coming closer. So, creating accountability, raising awareness and opening up choices are all open to you as ways to better serve your client and these are typical elements of coaching.

4. As we saw at the beginning of this chapter, your client may have developed thinking or behavioural habits that could or will be an obstacle or threat to their goals or quality of life. When working in a transactional way practitioners often see no or little value in helping clients have a healthy relationship with money. However, with level three client-centred relationships it is important because the focus is upon the client's wellbeing.

When you are truly client centred and conducting level three conversations then it is inevitable that you will see these kinds of situation crop up regularly in the course of your work.

Paul's story

Paul is one of my long-term coaching clients and is the co-owner and managing director of a company that has grown from three to over a hundred employees and that now has a significant turnover. From the outside it looked as though he was doing well; he lives in a substantial house and drives an expensive car. However, the truth was that his finances were in a delicate state and he was carrying a significant amount of long-term personal debt, which he kept adding to every time he got a pay rise.

During our coaching sessions Paul shared with me that he wanted to create more financial security for himself and his family and he could see that his debt levels were a problem. I asked him if this was something he felt was important enough to commit to doing something about and he said it was, so we agreed to some specific coaching on this issue.

In a coaching situation you are not the expert and do not need to come up with the answers for your client. Coaching is about raising someone's awareness. An analogy I often use with my clients is to ask them to imagine they had never seen a flame before and upon seeing one for the first time they, through curiosity, go and stick their finger in it. I ask them what would happen and, obviously, they say they would remove their finger from the flame pretty darn quickly! They would also immediately have a level of awareness about fire that they did not have before.

I ask them what might happen if they saw a flame again. Would they, for instance, need a motivational speaker to help them avoid putting their finger in it again? Would they need an expert's seven-step process or to join a support group to help them to avoid future flames? Clearly not, because it is the awareness that does all the work.

As a coach you are not responsible for your client's outcome. They are. You cannot afford to take on that burden because it will contaminate your thinking and lower your ability to make an impact. Your job is to show up fully and facilitate your client's having their own realisations.

Once Paul was able to share his situation he began to feel relieved of the burden he had been carrying, so this was already a shift for him. Listening to someone, without judgement, is an incredibly powerful process (and something that cannot be done if there is a hidden agenda). Over our coaching sessions I simply asked questions and listened. My intention was for Paul to experience a new level of awareness and I knew that, as a result, he would stop sticking his finger in the flame, which is what happened.

It also happened to be the case that Paul had a financial adviser who had arranged various financial products for him over the years. However, his adviser had never questioned why he was carrying so much debt. I am not offering up criticism of his financial adviser because as far as I know he had done a good job with the arrangements he had made. However, I am pointing to the fact that there was potential for him to open up a dialogue and assist his client further. From the adviser's perspective this could also have been potentially lucrative because the company was paying me a significant amount of money each month for the coaching sessions and the client clearly wanted help with the issue.

I do appreciate that not all practitioners will want to coach clients, however, if you are developing a truly client-centred practice then creating a mechanism to address such issues can be a valuable addition to what you offer in terms of genuine support for your clients.

What are your opportunities?

Unless you have already explored the kind of relationship that each of your clients has with money then there is almost certainly a wealth of untapped potential within your business. It can be remarkably simple to open up a dialogue and if you go back and review the questions in 'The art of discovery' chapter (Chapter 8), then asking some of these will start to bring a client's relationship with money up to the surface.

A simple example of opening a dialogue with a client could be:

You: 'Can I ask you a couple of questions about your relationship with money?'

Upon gaining permission your next question could be:

'On a scale of one to ten, with ten being high, how would you rate your relationship with money?'

If your client says 'What do you mean?' you can explain that you have come across many people, even those with a great deal of money, who spend far more time than is necessary worrying about it or being preoccupied with it, and this lowers their quality of life.

It may surprise you how low many people will score themselves on this kind of question but let's say that someone gives you a score of six, then your next question could be:

'If you could score yourself an eight, nine or even ten, then what would be different or what would you need to change?'

'And how would this make you feel?'

This simple line of questioning can really begin to open things up and, even if your client is not initially interested or motivated to do anything about it, you have been professional by asking and will have sown a seed. Many times I have sown seeds with my clients and they have, unprompted, brought up the subject at a later date.

The shift for the practitioner to make is seeing that the value in their client relationships is in the conversations rather than the transactions. All the time that advisers continue to be focused upon transactions then the aperture of how they see they can help clients will remain narrow. Once the broader perspective of life goals, living an authentic life and wellbeing is embraced then opportunities will be seen all over the place.

Thoughts to reflect on

The future of financial services lies in the holistic view of helping clients have a healthy relationship with money.

Leading practitioners will be able to coach as well as advise their clients.

Coaching represents a significant potential revenue stream for your practice.

Opportunities to have a broader conversation are already there, waiting for you to open them up.

The shift for the practitioner to make is seeing that the value in their client relationships is in the conversations rather than the transactions.

Chapter 11

What could stop you?

Chapter 11 – What could stop you?

Our doubts are traitors, and make us lose the good we oft might win, by fearing to attempt. **William Shakespeare**

Recently I was watching with delight as my little one-year-old niece Rosie was learning to walk. She would hold onto something, pull herself up, and then take a step or two before tumbling over. She would then get straight back up and have another go, again and again. A couple of weeks later, when I next saw her, she was still at it but this time taking several steps before losing control and going over. Despite her repeated attempts there was never a hint of frustration. In fact, she was full of joy because you could see her thinking 'I now have transport and I'm going places!'

Persistence, tenacity and resilience are built into us. We do not have to learn these things, we already have them in bundles. So why, as adults, do we often hesitate?

As we grow up and develop an ego we become afraid of failure. We fear trying something new in case we look stupid or our expectations are not met. Therefore, we give up too soon or never even try in the first place because of our insecurity.

Some advisers are reluctant to transition to having deeper and more meaningful conversations with their clients. They are fine having conversations about products, investments and financial situations but uncomfortable about having conversations that get more emotive.

One of the most liberating realisations that we can have is that we do not have to let our insecure thinking and self-doubt stop us doing what we want to do in life. If we are trying something new then how can we possibly expect to be proficient at it to begin with? I remember Michael Neill, one of the best success coaches in the world saying 'If you want to get really good at something then be willing to look bad more often!'

The thing to realise is that all of us have insecure thinking. It is not that some people have it and some don't. I have coached some extraordinarily successful people and they have self-doubt just like everybody else. The difference is that they have realised that they do not have to let their thinking control them, and what happens when we pay less attention to our insecure thinking is that it shows up far less often.

Having a better understanding of how we live entirely in a thought-created reality is what begins to set us free from the grasp of our fearful thinking. It is extremely helpful to understand that when we are anxious, insecure or fearful of change then our imaginations will often run wild, filling in the void of uncertainty with outcomes that look bad to us. This is precisely the time to understand that our thinking is unreliable and distorted and we do not have to take it seriously.

As fearful thinking so often looks like reality rather than thinking, it is useful to look at how this kind of thinking can show up, so that you can recognise it when it does. Clearly, whilst not a complete list, these are the reasons that advisers avoid having powerful, emotional conversations that I have heard again and again:

'I don't know how to have deeper, more emotional conversations with my clients.'

Advisers totally underestimate their ability to have powerful conversations with their clients. If we feel insecure then it looks as if we do not know what to do. However, this is a state-of-mind issue and not a skills or knowledge issue.

Of course, you gain experience and learn as you go along but when you have the intention of truly understanding your client and discovering what they want from life then you will be surprised at how well this intention will carry you through.

In fifteen years of having deeper conversations with my clients, both as an adviser and subsequently as a coach, the experiences and results have always been positive. In literally thousands of hours of deeper conversations I cannot remember anyone objecting and most people are more than willing to talk about what really matters to them.

'I am doing fine as I am; I don't need to have these kinds of conversations.'

Practitioners can, of course, make a living by simply focusing on products and financial situations and yet by doing this they are missing out on making their work truly life-changing for their clients and far more deeply fulfilling and rewarding for themselves.

True financial planning can only be based upon having a thorough understanding of your client and nothing less will do. If you were to ask practitioners who operate at the deeper level if they would go back to being transactional the answer you would hear is that it would just not make sense to them.

'I don't like all this touchy-feely stuff.'

As mentioned earlier, many advisers are comfortable talking about products, investments and financial matters but very uncomfortable with more meaningful conversations. If you keep your work on an analytical, intellectual level then the degree of your client's emotional engagement, which is where the real value resides, will rarely reach anywhere near its true potential.

Your own uncomfortable feelings are not a valid reason for avoiding working at a deeper level. It is not about how you feel; it is about serving your client as deeply as you can.

'It's uncomfortable!'

Any discomfort is coming from your own thinking and not the situation. When you put your attention fully on your client, especially by listening at level three with nothing on your mind, you will find that any uncomfortable feelings you have will simply fade away. Very soon you will develop a high level of inner confidence and wonder why you didn't do it sooner.

'My clients won't like it.'

This is mind reading and a generalised comment usually based upon an adviser's insecurity. It may be true that some people might not want to have a deeper conversation, just the same as many people do not want to have conversations about financial products and investments.

My experience, and the experience of my adviser clients who operate at level three, is that the vast majority of people are very willing to engage in a meaningful conversation about themselves and what they want. They just need you to give them the opportunity.

'It takes too long!'

The right clients will be more than willing to have powerful conversations, so taking too long is not an issue.

In fact, many advisers are far too quick to rush in and want to give advice. Slowing down and taking your client conversations to a deeper level will be the best thing you ever do. There is no activity you can engage in that will deliver more value to your clients than the quality of conversation that you engage them in.

An ideal client may well be with you for many years and could be worth five or even six figures in revenue. Putting in more up front will pay huge dividends to your business.

The foundation of client-centred relationships

In Chapter 1 we looked at some of the comparisons between healthy psychological functioning and unhealthy psychological functioning. All the vital aspects of level three relationships that we have explored in this section of the chapter have their foundation in healthy functioning.

Your clarity of mind is what facilitates a rich, engaging and transformational experience for your clients because it promotes their healthy psychological functioning. When you have the willingness to hold a space for your clients and they experience free-flowing, intuitive thinking then they will not only feel deeply touched, they too will experience incredible clarity of mind. Nothing will hold more value than this for your clients because it is the foundation of everything that follows.

Thoughts to reflect on

The vast majority of clients will find enormous value in exploring what they really want from life.

The only thing that can stop you having level three conversations is paying too much attention to self-doubt and insecure thinking.

Self-doubt often shows up in ways that look real, so do not be fooled.

When we pay less attention to our self-doubt it fades away.

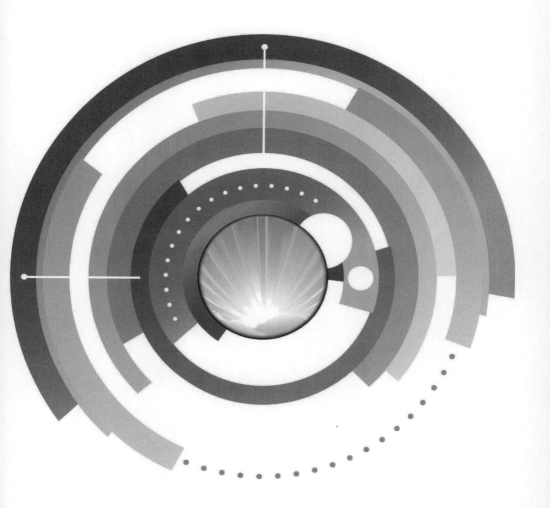

Section 3

Masters at work: five successful client-centred advisers share their philosophy

In this section five successful client-centred advisers share their philosophy and approach to working with their clients. Their businesses vary in size from small to medium, each has its own approach and yet all are completely client centred. You will get a sense from each contributor about the most important values of their business, what they do for clients and why it makes sense to them to operate as they do. This will create a practical context for what we have been talking about so far and help you to think about how you can develop your business, in your own way.

Chapter 12

How my father's
paperwork inspired me
to build a company

Dominic Baldwin
Xentum IFA

Chapter 12 – How my father's paperwork inspired me to build a company

Dominic Baldwin founded Xentum IFA in 2004. Based in Lymm and London, Xentum now looks after a select group of clients throughout the UK, as well as working with some of the country's biggest firms of solicitors and accountants. In this chapter Dominic talks about the personal story behind the company, Xentum's philosophy and how they look after their clients.

It was the spring of 2004. I was going through my father's paperwork. He wasn't well and for the first time this proud man had let me take charge of his finances. 'Mess' wasn't an adequate word.

I found plans, policies and investments. Whatever the financial services industry had invented, Dad had one. The trouble was, every plan, policy or investment had been funded by the surrender of its predecessor. The procession of plausible men in suits that had called to see Dad had done very well indeed: the commissions had been significant. What they'd left behind wasn't.

My growing discontent with the financial services industry started to crystallise. I realised there was only one ethical decision I could make. So, I went to see the MD of the company I worked for.

'I'm sorry, Dominic. For a minute there I thought you said you were only going to be paid by fees.'

'I did. A hundred per cent. No commission – ever.'

'You're an idiot,' the MD said. 'We'll see you back here in a year's time. After you've had to sell your house and your car.'

And that was that. I'd resigned. I was no longer a director of a firm that was doing very well out of commissions. I'd committed myself to starting Xentum: committed myself to starting a financial services company that was going to be completely open, completely ethical and run in the interests of the clients, not the sales targets.

It was, if you like, a perfect storm. Three years earlier I'd bought Moss Wood: my dream home – a 1930s house in the Cheshire countryside, built by an eccentric Canadian millionaire and modelled on an East African tea plantation. But it had been neglected for 20 years – and now I had a new business to build. It was hard explaining to my wife that I couldn't fix the roof because I needed to see a client. Stress levels were high. What else could we add to the mix?

'I'm pregnant,' my wife said...

Last November Xentum celebrated its tenth birthday. We were joined at Moss Wood by 60 clients, friends and professional connections. It was a truly wonderful day – my only sadness was that my dad wasn't there to see it. He'd finally lost his battle with cancer in September 2009.

But I hope he'd have been proud of what we've created. Xentum is now a team of ten dealing with clients throughout the UK from offices in Lymm and London. Everyone who works for the company owns a part of it. I'm pleased to say that in the ten years since we opened our doors we have never once accepted a commission payment. We've always been paid by fees, our clients have received the same advice irrespective of the amount they had to invest and no – I didn't have to sell my house or my car.

I've never had to set a sales target for anyone in the Xentum team – and I never will. I've always believed that if you put the client and your ethical values front and centre then the 'sales' – if that's the word you want to use – will come naturally.

Do I feel any satisfaction that the rest of the financial services industry has now been compelled to join us? That scandal after mis-selling scandal has finally brought about legislation that led to the end of commission and a move to fee-based advice? No, I don't. I simply feel sad that we're still seeing new clients who've received the same advice my father received: 'switch everything you've got because it will generate commission and help me meet my targets.'

Xentum, however, prospers. I'm proud to say that I work with some of the best-qualified and most professional financial planners in the UK. But as Theodore Roosevelt said 'People don't care how much you know until they know how much you care.' And that pretty much sums us up – we know a lot, but we care a lot more.

So how do we deal with our clients? Let me walk you through the process…

Potential clients typically come to us in one of three ways: they might be introduced to us by existing clients, or the meeting may be at the suggestion of the client's professional advisers. Alternatively, they may have been invited or brought along to one of our events at Moss Wood. But wherever the introduction has come from the first meeting is always the same. I simply go along and meet them – and the key word at the meeting is 'understanding'.

I want to understand what they want to achieve in life, what really 'floats their boat' – or if you want to put it in management-speak, what are their key drivers? And no, I'm not talking about financial planning, I'm talking about family life.

'I want to make sure my family continues to benefit from the business I've built.'

'I want to make sure there's enough money to buy the children a house and pay for my daughter's wedding.'

'I want to pay for my grandson's education.'

Any financial planning we ultimately do is simply a way of helping our client achieve these goals. I'm happy to drink my tea and listen.

The client needs to understand us as well. Do they understand what Xentum can do to help? Do they appreciate how we'll add value? Do they understand – and are they happy with – our values and philosophy?

The first meeting, and the understanding it generates, is absolutely crucial. I've built Xentum on long-term relationships, not short-term sales and I will never deviate from that.

The meeting may take a long time, I think my record is five and a half hours, but it's the basis of our relationship; a relationship founded on a lot of tea and a lot of listening.

All the detailed work happens at the second meeting. That's the one where we gather the hard facts: investments, savings, pensions and so on. Very often we'll need to do a lot of work after the second meeting – writing off to insurance and investment companies for up-to-date valuations and so on – but that's all part and parcel of comprehensive financial planning. We can't advise a client how to achieve their aims and ambitions until we know where they're starting from.

Eventually, we'll have a full picture – and now comes the moment which, even after ten years, gives me the most satisfaction.

Our clients are Xentum clients. They're not my clients or David's or Adam's or Sam's. I'd seen that too many times at my previous firm. 'Jim's left now: I'm looking after all your investments. And you know what, Mr Smith? I think I'd suggest a few changes…' The very words that had cost my father so much money.

We take a 'whole team' approach to our clients' financial planning, and if there's one factor that's contributed to our success, that's it.

Half a dozen of us sit round the boardroom table: David, Adam, our two Sams, Claire – who's our head of administration and responsible for putting whatever we decide into practice – and me. We discuss our client's aims and objectives, where they are now and where they want to be. We bounce ideas around and we may draw on our experience of existing clients with similar situations.

Between us, the members of our advisory team have a huge range of expertise. Just as importantly, we have a range of personalities. As you might expect, I'm always ready to empathise with the client. David, our head of financial planning and one of the technical experts in the financial services industry, is more pragmatic. Everyone contributes their expertise and their individual insights.

The discussion will continue until everyone is happy that we have arrived at the very best solution. Then, and only then, will we make a recommendation to our client.

The beauty of this approach is that it guarantees absolute continuity in a client's financial planning. If one of our team were to leave, it wouldn't matter: the client's path has already been mapped out by the whole team. There is simply no possibility of anyone at Xentum recommending changes in a client's portfolio for their own benefit.

We'll then meet with the client and – more often than not – their other professional advisers, and if everyone is happy Claire and her administration team put the plans into practice and schedule the regular follow-up meetings.

That approach clearly works: it's earned us the loyalty of our wonderful clients, every one of whom I am delighted to call a personal friend. It's earned us the respect of an ever-widening pool of solicitors, accountants and other professional colleagues who entrust us with their clients' financial planning – and it's enabled us to become the 'financial director' for some of the wealthiest families in Cheshire and the surrounding counties.

Let me finish where I began – with a story. My client, whose name I've obviously changed, was John Brown. John was an old school family GP: he'd been married to Joan for 30 years and they had two daughters, both now at university. John was one of my original clients who'd come with me when I'd left the previous firm to establish Xentum. I'd known him for 20 years or more.

We were sitting in his garden, looking out over the Cheshire countryside and finishing a gin and tonic. I'd brought him up to date on the progress of his investments, but as we always did, we'd spent far more time talking about the progress of his garden.

'You'll have to keep an eye on it for me, Dom,' he said.

'I always do, John,' I said, not immediately catching the change in his voice.

'No,' he said. 'You'll really have to keep an eye on it for me. And Joan and the girls. I've got cancer.'

I simply didn't know what to say. I stammered some useless words about treatment, chemo, radiotherapy…

John shook his head. 'Gone too far,' he said. 'I might see Christmas.'

In the event John didn't see Christmas. But in the time he had left we were able to plan absolutely everything. He died knowing that his wife would be secure in the home they'd both loved so much, that money was set aside for his daughters' weddings and that the future of the grandchildren he'd never see would be secure.

I see Joan twice a year now. We sit in the garden and drink a gin and tonic in remembrance and she shows me the pictures of her first grandchild.

Joan – and a hundred clients like her – is the reason I do what I do. She's the reason I'll never need an alarm clock in the morning. Our clients are why I started Xentum, why I founded it with the principles I did and why those principles will never change.

Chapter 13

They won't remember
what you said; they will
remember how you
made them feel

Andy Jervis
Chesterton House
Financial Planning Ltd

Chapter 13 – They won't remember what you said; they will remember how you made them feel

Andy Jervis is co-owner of Chesterton House Financial Planning, based in Loughborough. Andy's mission has been to develop a financial planning practice that is a recognised leader in the field, which he has unquestionably accomplished. The practice consistently achieves outstanding scores for delivering work of exceptional quality coupled with great client service and support.

'That,' I exclaimed with finality in my voice, 'would give me great satisfaction!'

I leaned back slightly. I had reached the top of my Values Staircase. I was done.

But Mitch took me by surprise, because *he* wasn't done. He looked at me with deep interest, and as he spoke his whole body was alive with anticipation.

'What I want to know, Andy, what I really want to know, is: what's important about experiencing that sense of great satisfaction to you?'

He really wanted to know. I thought hard. My head started to spin. Then suddenly all became clear. I began to shake. I had never experienced anything like this before.

We were both attending Bill Bachrach's Values-Based Financial Planning Academy in San Diego, California. We were practising the Values Conversation that is at the core of Bill's teaching, and I had experienced it many times before. At each Academy we rehearsed it maybe 20 times, and I was on my fifth visit. But Mitch Harris was a multiple attender, and it showed. At this Academy I had been asked the same question over and over again by a succession of delegates, and each time I had reached that point, with the same finality in my voice, they took my cue and stopped. We both knew I'd got to the top.

But not Mitch. No, it took this man from Northampton, 40 miles from my office in Loughborough, in a meeting on the other side of the world, to take me to a whole new place.

If you've never experienced this type of conversation – and unless you've attended a course like this I'm guessing you haven't – then you won't have the faintest idea what I'm talking about.

Which is a shame, because neither will you have experienced the immense power that emanates from getting in touch with what's profoundly important to you. Understanding yourself in this way is not only hugely motivating, it's also eerily reassuring. Knowing that you are being completely you, fully authentic and unadulterated, leads to a sense of peace and tranquillity that I can't easily put into words.

You'll also never have known the way in which this sort of conversation transforms relationships, and not just business ones. Try asking your partner or best friend what's truly important to them, and then listen. Dig, and listen more. Go deeper, deeper and deeper still. Ask the questions no one else ever asked them. Don't judge, don't problem solve, don't advise, just listen. You'll be amazed by what you both learn.

This is at the heart of my work with clients. Of course, as a qualified and experienced financial planner they look to me to understand the vagaries of tax, investment, pensions and savings. They expect me to tell them where to put their money, how to structure their finances, their businesses and their personal affairs to get the best returns. So far, so commonplace.

But that's not where the value in our relationship resides. It's not what creates wealth, what makes that wealth meaningful, or what gives them profound peace of mind around money. No, that comes from their behaviour.

I realised long ago that influencing behavioural change is the very essence of great financial planning. And there's plenty of evidence to support this assertion. The long-running Dalbar study (www.dalbar.com) in the US shows that the returns most do-it-yourself investors receive from their portfolios are far less than they could be getting, and this is a direct result of their own errant behaviour. The reasons are clear – they get pulled along by their emotions and end up systematically selling too low and buying too high, missing the best periods of investment returns that ever-changing markets offer by trying to predict the unpredictable. Yet the clear evidence shows that simply leaving their investments alone and resisting the urge to dabble can add as much as 6 per cent a year to returns over a 20-year period – the difference between a comfortable and prosperous retirement and penury.

This is a point that unfortunately is completely missed by many otherwise highly competent financial advisers, who believe that their role is to pick the best investments, help structure portfolios and save on the costs of investing, among other things. Yet the long-term effects of these activities, important as they are, pales into insignificance compared to the adviser's central function of keeping their client on track and helping apply a long-term discipline to a long-term activity. If your investments are there to fund your retirement, the reality is that they will probably never be cashed in your lifetime, and decisions should be made in the light of this revelation.

There are countless examples of behaviour as the crucial element in financial success. Repeatedly I've seen that it's not the return on the investment that's important so much as whether the investment was ever made in the first place. It's not how you invest for your children that's by far the greatest factor in their future financial success so much as the example you set for them today. And it's not the interest charged on that loan that will keep you from wealth as much as whether you decide to take out the loan in the first place.

Influencing these sorts of decisions is a vital part of the job specification for any financial planner who truly cares about helping his or her clients to achieve financial freedom. The adviser who restricts himself to technical issues only is doing his or her clients a great disservice.

And how do you exert this kind of influence? In my experience there is only one sure way. Focus on what's deeply important, and let your client come to his or her own realisation in a state of intense clarity.

Doing this means asking the right questions, and listening to the answer without comment. This last point is so important I'll say it again. Without comment.

The natural human inclination is to 'guide' and 'advise'. We like to think we're helping. But in reality the power in conversation is in simply being there and allowing a person to come to their own realisation, unaided – except by your presence.

Of course, if you're a technician and proud of it you'll dismiss all of this as touchy-feely mumbo-jumbo that has no place in the real world. You'll probably continue to give your clients first-class advice that will, if followed, take them most efficiently to their goal.

But you won't inspire them.

I had one such conversation with my client, David. We were exploring what was important to him. 'So what I would really like to know,' I told David, 'is: what's important about knowing that you are helping your family in the way that you describe, to you?'

David reflected in silence. I recognised the inner searching that was taking place as he worked to come up with his answer. I'd seen it many times before.

The silence seemed to last for hours.

Eventually David spoke. 'Because,' he said softly, 'I would be fulfilling a promise I made to myself many years ago to never treat my kids the way I was treated by my father.'

I knew that David had revealed something to me that he had shared with very few people in his life. I didn't ask him to explain, there was no need. This had been a deep revelation for David, and I simply allowed the moment to settle.

'What do we need to do?' he asked quietly.

The work we did together thereafter took on new meaning for both of us. David knew at his own deepest level what his financial plan was about, and guided by this knowledge there was a subtle but profound shift in his approach. At future meetings he was perceptibly calmer, more focused, more relaxed and more open to ideas. His plan developed rapidly and his portfolio grew strongly. Don't ask me how it works, but I'm convinced that there is a positive link between the returns someone generates from their investments and the degree of commitment they demonstrate in building it. Life helps those who help themselves.

Your clients won't experience these revelations without you as their coach as well as their financial adviser, and you won't be in a position to create that experience without a coach of your own. I've been told many times by advisers as I speak to them at meetings across the UK that 'I already ask deep questions of my clients'. Yet their very way of being demonstrates that they don't understand what I'm trying to tell them. Their minds are closed.

So if you want to build your skills in this most vital area, my advice is: find a great coach, pay their astronomical fees (never choose your coach on price), and do the exercises they set you. Let them take you to places you've never been and answer questions you've never been asked. Learn to live your life in a way that's inspiring to you, your clients and the people you love and who love you.

That's what I did, and the rewards have been immeasurable, not just in monetary terms. I've learned from some great teachers and I've discovered things about myself that I would never have really known without their help.

Thanks Mitch, and many other great people like you. You helped me find the real me. I'll always be grateful.

And I know that I'm a far better financial planner and that my clients are in a much better place because of it.

Chapter 14

How to deliver great value for the fees you want to charge

**Nik Proctor
Lodgeport Associates
Ltd**

Chapter 14 – How to deliver great value for the fees you want to charge

Nik Proctor formed Lodgeport Associates Limited, based in Leatherhead, Surrey, in 2001 to specialise in lifestyle financial planning. He has designed specialised programmes including the Lifestyle Achievement Programme and Entrepreneurs Exit Strategy to help clients focus upon and achieve their desired lifestyle. Clients find Nik's ability to explain complex wealth protection, legal and investment issues in an easy and entertaining way very refreshing.

We have been very fortunate to receive valuable guidance from some of the financial planning professions' leading practitioners. This guidance has given us the confidence to change our business model and approach to financial planning in many different ways. One of our guiding principles with new clients and projects for existing clients is 'Can we deliver great value for the fees we want to charge and still have the work be profitable to us?'

Delivering great value to your clients comes from being interested in helping them and gaining a thorough understanding of their circumstances and finding out what they want to accomplish. This involves asking great questions. Asking their permission to ask your questions is really important because the client needs to feel comfortable with you and prepared to share the answers to those searching questions.

To our clients, a successful outcome is finding people they can trust and have confidence in who will help them define what their priorities are and create a plan that they can see is achievable. This gives them a greater sense of confidence, a greater sense of direction and a greater feeling of capability.

The importance of mutually agreed value

We were recently contacted by a person who attended one of our seminars five years ago. He said that he had been so impressed by our approach that he had told his wife that when they had enough money they would get in contact with my firm to help them plan their future.

Prior to our meeting together the couple had returned our client profile (a brief financial snapshot of their situation) to assist us in making our time together more valuable. It also helps them to focus their minds on the things that will be important when planning their future.

An hour into the meeting, during which I had shared my concerns about the magnitude of their goals, given their timescales, I stopped talking and paused. After a few moments I explained my concern. One of our guiding principles is to provide great value for money and I was not feeling confident that we would be able to achieve that result. This some-what surprised the couple as it was not a reaction they were expecting. My message here is, that despite all the time we had invested so far and the help I had given them, I was willing to walk away from a potential new client relationship because I doubted we could give them great value for the fees we would have needed to charge to be profitable.

Delivering a comprehensive lifestyle financial planning service is very time consuming for us. This is mainly due to the breadth of topics we cover in our discussions, the level of detail we go into and the time we give clients to carefully think through their answers.

After further discussion the clients said they thought our services would be very valuable. We agreed to write to them summarising their key issues, our fees and what would happen if they decided to instruct us over the first year and beyond. As it turned out, the couple advised us that they were going to delay instructing us, however, I was not disappointed because I do not want to take on clients unless they are wholly convinced of the value we can bring to them.

Our main mission is to help clients achieve financial independence and their desired lifestyle for themselves and their families, help them focus on their priorities in life and help them do so in a way our clients genuinely value.

Alan and Barbara

Another of our guiding principles is being able to advise on the whole of a client's circumstances and finances, rather than just one particular area. Through our holistic approach, both the clients and ourselves are able to see 'the bigger picture' and, therefore, clearer and more beneficial decisions can be made.

Alan and Barbara were a married couple who wanted to improve their lifestyle, yet without really understanding their circumstances, what they wanted to accomplish and their concerns, we wouldn't have been able to help them as much as we did.

Their business is a seasonal one with a large part of their revenue being generated at Christmas and in the summer. Offering competitive prices is very important so they were concerned about increasing their turnover and exceeding the VAT threshold as this would make their prices uncompetitive. So, increasing their income could not be achieved through the current business. Faced with this challenge, together we examined their strengths and opportunities and moved them into the area of strategic planning.

We explored the possibility of Alan setting up a separate consultancy business advising other small traders using his extensive skills in importing goods, sourcing supplies from the UK and overseas, knowledge of the application process for trade and charity fairs, and experience in how to plan, prepare and maximise attendance at exhibitions and fairs. They also had good connections with key people at trade organisations of which they were members. This would give them great introductions to potential clients. Also no one else was offering this service!

This kind of conversation is much more in depth than simply focusing on financial arrangements and clients get real value from it. In this case Alan left the meeting saying he was really excited about developing this plan and Barbara found it much more positive than she had been expecting. Not surprisingly, they were very happy to renew their membership of our programme and accept our increased fees.

Charlie and Rachel

We have found over the years that creating a family tree for clients of relatives together with notes on their current circumstances can be very valuable. It acts as a useful reminder in meetings when discussing opportunities for families to help each other. Against this background and a determination to help our clients focus on their priorities, the value we can bring is not only clear but often considerable.

Clients of fifteen years standing, Charlie and Rachel, have achieved a number of important life goals for themselves and their family by working closely with us.

They have run a very profitable business from home for 18 years as agents for an American electronics company, selling their products to UK companies. One of their goals was to bring their son and daughter-in-law into their business, whilst ensuring that their own financial future was still secure.

We worked together to produce a detailed lifetime cash-flow model of their future lifestyle. This demonstrated to them how they could financially benefit their children now, whilst still maintaining their long-term financial security. The effect of gifting money to the children so they could pay down mortgages, gave the children more disposable income. We also advised them how they could use these funds through a salary exchange process to create tax savings from which the family company would invest in pension plans for the children. The improvement to their children's future retirement security was really appealing to them.

The challenge the following year for Charlie and Rachel was how to help their daughter and her husband move to a bigger house nearer the family business. Their son-in-law had recently started work for the family business and had a three-hour commute. The couple had also recently had another child and were bursting at the seams of their house.

We showed Charlie and Rachel how they could afford to sell an investment property and gift most of the money, via the family gifting structure we set up, to their daughter so that she and her husband could afford to move into a bigger house closer to the office. All this was achieved without the parents significantly reducing their future financial security. We also agreed to explain the proposal to their son so that he did not feel unfairly treated.

Essentially the message we conveyed was that the family would look after their priorities first and do what they could to help each other. Monetary imbalances would be sorted out in the future. As you would imagine everyone was delighted with our advice, especially Charlie and Rachel who were now confidently able to help their children.

The real value that we bring to clients is helping them focus on their priorities and make important decisions with confidence. This is partly achieved by taking the time to discuss their options and the consequences of those choices. Their lifetime cash-flow model is a key tool in this process. It can take more time and effort on our part to get to the core issues but doing so can be genuinely life-changing, as it was in this case.

Jackie

Good financial planning is not always about growing the money for the future, it can be about what the money can do to improve lives now. A good example of this is our work with long-term client Jackie, a widow of eight years.

Jackie wasn't doing all the things she wanted to do with her life because money was tight following a significant drop in the rental income she received from her commercial property. This had resulted from the new terms of a renegotiated lease.

We reviewed our understanding of the relationships in her family and we asked her to examine all her outgoings carefully. With a very clear picture of her circumstances we were able to advise her to take a number of steps.

She stopped paying for some expensive insurance policies. There was one which covered the potential inheritance tax on her estate, which we arranged to be paid by her daughter and successful son-in-law. This led to them offering to pay our client's son's mortgage, which our client had been paying for several years. We advised her to accept this offer and how to structure the conversation to increase the likelihood of her daughter and son-in-law sticking to their offer.

We are also discussing the benefits of downsizing her home, moving nearer to her daughter and investing the equity released to further improve her income. If all goes to plan she will end up with more disposable income and be able to do all the things that she has so far been unable to do. Naturally she is very grateful for our help and the direction we have given her.

Even when clients discuss their worries and concerns with their spouses or family and friends, it is safe to say that no one else is in the position we are in to help. We have a complete picture of the client's finances. We are objective and understand the relevant technical issues. Also we are able to explain their options and the consequences as pictures of their future, using their cash-flow forecasts.

We feel pleased that we have made a significant difference in the lives of each of these families. Often, people can talk about the things that are important to them and what they would like to do with their lives but never get around to doing them. Through the time we invest in our clients and the trust we build we can take the quality and relevance of our work to another level, which is highly beneficial for our clients and their families as well as highly rewarding for us.

Chapter 15

How much value are
you adding?

Dominic Thomas
Solomons IFA

Chapter 15 – How much value are you adding?

Dominic Thomas founded Solomon's IFA, based in Raynes Park, South West London, in 1999 and was, at the time, one of very few advisers operating a proper fee system. The principles of Solomon's are transparency, integrity and accountability and testimony to this is the fact that the continued healthy growth of the business has been primarily through recommendation.

I passionately believe that financial planning is a game changer, a life changer. Arranging financial products is not. There is nothing terribly appealing about the prospect of a conversation about the worst things that could happen to you or your family or the mind-numbing frenetic keeping up with stock market reports and opinion. Many couples find it incredibly difficult to talk about money. Relate cites money as one of the major stresses in a relationship and often a significant factor in a broken one. Many people struggle with being honest about money, admitting that we aren't perfect or completely financially solvent is akin to confession, which few are willingly going to partake in, especially if there is little or no trust.

Any conversation about money has the possibility of raising some uncomfortable issues. At some point you will be asked about how you intend to provide for yourself and others, and how far along the path you have progressed. Many people, perhaps most, would prefer to avoid uncomfortable discussions because very few of us like to feel vulnerable or admit to not making good decisions. So let me begin by acknowledging that pitching up to an adviser's office takes a fair amount of courage.

The disconnect

I used to think that becoming an investment expert and creating risk-based portfolios would help to demonstrate my skill and knowledge, providing better returns to clients. The truth is it didn't. Selecting successful funds is not easy, these days I might even suggest it is implausible and probably irrelevant. I was still hung up on how well the portfolio, pension or ISA was performing. Yet how much of the performance, good or bad, was truly down to me? Was this what clients were paying fees for?

There was a huge disconnection between the money and the client – I was still often meeting the same glazed expressions of boredom, accompanied by anxiety about the future.

Financial planning is about creating a proper financial plan – which is, for want of a better expression, a route map to get you from where you are now, to where you want to go. It may not involve any advice about financial products (but it might). The focus is completely on the client, their journey and their destination. Precisely how they get there and what they need to do will be a type of action list – which probably involves financial products, but these are merely tools to do the job and deliver the results. When the client has a proper plan that's engaged with and which reflects their values and real-life situation, they have the framework on which to build choices.

Creating a clear direction

It's rather important to know what you are aiming for, what your goals are. Most people haven't articulated their goals clearly, even though they probably have some. This is where careful and thoughtful questions are needed. How you pose the questions is a real skill and one that needs to be learned. However, in the simplest form, we are trying to help clients address the question 'What do I really want and why?' The 'why' is not designed to be judgmental but to expose the client's motivation, thinking and values.

The adviser has no place challenging the client's personal values or motivation, however, the thinking part – well that may need to be discussed thoughtfully. For example, if a client believes that they will die by the time they are 65 so doesn't believe it's worth having a pension, that's thinking that needs discussion. If someone believes that cash is better than investment, they need to clearly understand what they are really getting into. If a client believes that inflation is a low number that's not worth worrying about… and so on.

In essence, you as your client's adviser need to check understanding and this may require some education, perhaps re-education. There is an awful lot of nonsense within the world of money and investing and being clear about what someone believes and why is important. Naturally, admitting that we don't know everything carries its own issues, so again the adviser needs an approach that is helpful, clear and not patronising. I see a large part of my role as an educator – helping people understand what their options are from a place of knowledge rather than fear or ignorance.

Cash-flow forecasting

A moment of personal enlightenment for me was triggered by a fortunate combination of years of experience and some major improvements in technology. I was able to use cash-flow forecasting as a tool to explore, with my clients, various scenarios of how the future might look.

Imagine flying from Heathrow to New York and starting your flight just a couple of degrees off track: unless the plane is brought back on course, you won't be landing in New York, but perhaps Caracas, Venezuela. The value of reviewing progress cannot be overstated because as time goes by things change (a lot!). For example, our governments regularly change tax rules, allowances and the economy, so understanding the impact of these changes is vital – but the message can be lost unless it can be easily and clearly demonstrated.

A great financial planner will model different scenarios, showing the impact of different decisions (and of not making decisions). How this can positively, and enormously, impact someone's life was clearly demonstrated with one of our clients. We initially had an in-depth discussion with the client about his values and what he would really like to do with his life. He admitted that he was fed up in his NHS career but had never considered leaving because he was worried about the effect on his pension. With detailed knowledge of the client's situation, using cash-flow modelling, we were able to show him how it was possible to take a year out and maintain the long-term benefits of his employment. The result was that he took the year out and went round the world – a long-held ambition and something that he had not seriously considered until we showed him it was possible.

One of the most basic things I do with clients these days is visually show them the practical benefit of proper budgeting, but not in a restrictive, straitjacket, diet-like way that we all know is unlikely to be followed for long. A proper budget is automated and liberating, but when followed, without doing anything complex, makes an enormous difference to a client's reserves and net worth. This enables clients to build bigger reserves, high-speed fund mortgages, and clear debt before building a robust investment portfolio to ensure that they don't run out of money and know what returns are required to achieve this.

Clients love this process because for the first time they can see that it's about them, their lives and choices, not about financial products. It also enables them to have greater confidence in starting to give money away to their children or charities. This may sound like a small thing, but think about it for a moment. Most people don't see their children or charities benefit from their gifts until they die – in which case it's too late to see the impact. Most advisers operate in a world of accumulating wealth, where more is better. However, you cannot take it with you and being able to gift funds without damaging your own financial security is hugely rewarding and satisfying to both donor and recipient.

A litmus test you might want to consider is to ask 'How much value am I adding?'

An adviser may be tempted to discuss their ability to pick outperforming investments or their ability to offer discounts on investment costs or talk about percentage points. In contrast, by understanding what is really important to the client, what their values are and also, what their genuine concerns are, we can specifically address these. In our experience this adds tremendous value because the client can see it is all about them. Through looking at the client's behaviour, opening up choices and clearly demonstrating the implications of different decisions we often add significant financial value to our clients' net worth. This can often sound like an outrageous figure, as an example, this week I prepared a very simple financial plan which, if followed, will improve our client's net worth by nearly £3m over 20 years. It sounds like a ludicrous amount, but it's about doing the maths properly, following a clear budget and getting rid of debt and mortgages.

Ultimately, when clients instinctively know it is all about them it creates a deep bond of trust and a collaborative way of working together. We find that this enables us to create results that really matter to people and thus ensures long-term relationships that are both profitable and help our business to experience continued healthy growth.

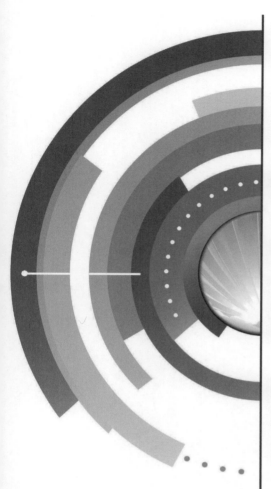

Chapter 16

Why a client-centric approach is the only way to operate our financial practice

Paul Tracy
Provest Financial
Solutions

Chapter 16 – Why a client-centric approach is the only way to operate our financial practice

Paul Tracey has built Provest Financial Planning purely by referral. The business joined St. James's Place Wealth Management in 2008 as a partner practice. Paul is exceptionally committed to continually improving and evolving the service they give to clients, which is why Provest is highly valued by its clients and continues to grow healthily.

Since I established Provest Financial Solutions, a successful financial planning practice in Barnt Green, West Midlands, the company has become a huge advocate of lifestyle financial planning. The lifestyle approach to financial planning is now integral to how we run our business and relies on placing the needs of clients first.

Moving financial services from a product-centric to a client-centric industry is just a no-brainer in terms of the enormous benefits gained for both the client and the financial practice. The reasons for this I will try to articulate, as I explain the process we use from the moment a client contacts us for advice to the completion of their financial plan.

Discovery comes first

Our first stage in working with a new client is to hold an initial discovery meeting and at this stage, we determine what's important to the client. To devise a detailed financial plan fully linked to a client's real needs, values and desires, we ask clients fundamental questions that often get them thinking about their life goals fully for the first time. We also help them to find the deeper meaning and motivation behind their goals, before prioritising them. The fundamental questions we ask them include 'what do you want to do with the rest of your life?' and 'how much will it cost?'

This conversation can become serious at times. If they knew they only had a few years left before their demise, what would be on their 'bucket list'? Spending more time with their family is usually at the top of the list but it may not be. Unless we understand a client at a deep level, it's difficult to tailor a financial plan to their exact needs.

As well as any immediate concerns, the number one question I am asked by potential clients is how much money they need to be OK and achieve what they want out of life. Therefore, if we weren't thorough enough at the discovery stage, this would be an impossible question to answer. After all, one person's definition of 'OK' is very different to another's.

If they have the money they need, we urge them to carry on living their life. If not, we can help them address this. Our objective is to help clients gain more time and a better quality of life by providing them with more choices and freedom, as well as feelings of security and peace of mind. This is gained through clarity of their finances and understanding where they are heading.

In terms of attitudes to money, we encourage people not to worry about what they have no control over, such as interest rates, markets and inflation. Instead, we urge them to focus on what they can control, such as determining their goals and maintaining discipline. I strongly believe that this is a great philosophy for life in general. Importantly, we also encourage clients to take lower levels of risk. Why take more risks than you need to with investments, for example, if it doesn't align with your life goals?

Importantly, at this early stage, we also determine whether we actually like the client, understand their values and whether we feel we can establish trust. Can we help solve their problems? The best client relationships are those built on mutual respect and understanding. We need clients to be completely open and honest with us if they are to really benefit from the process of working with us. If we feel that the client is not suitable we will politely explain that we don't think that our service can add value to them and introduce them to another suitable adviser within our network.

Helping clients gain clarity

Sometimes, clients don't understand what they want out of life until we ask and they take the time to consider it. One thing is for sure, they certainly don't want a lower standard of living than they have now, so our main objective may be to protect what they already have.

For example, one worried 69-year-old client was referred to us by his daughter. He was concerned about a mortgage he had to pay off on a buy-to-let property within the following two years. After he passed away, he also wanted to ensure the security of his wife and children. His son had a property in negative equity and he wondered if he was in a position to help him. By fully understanding the client and his situation, we were able to show him that he had options – taking him from uncertainty to certainty. Similarly to most clients, he had found himself constantly worrying about his financial problems. Ultimately, we aim to offer such clients peace of mind.

Determining the key numbers

Using what we've learned from the discovery stage, we are better able to understand the position of a family and a business, including assets and liabilities, as well as their values and objectives. An essential aspect of our work is determining a client's key numbers. This is the money they need to ensure they never run out; often it is their number one concern. It is also the amount of money they need to achieve their goals over their estimated lifetime. Clearly, every individual has a different 'number', so to get the numbers right, a client's lifestyle goals must be fully understood. How well we understand their goals is dependent on the quality and depth of our communication with them, which places a whole new level of importance on effective communication and relationship building.

Following plenty of research, a tailored financial plan that usually includes multiple strands of finances, such as savings and pensions will be integrated to follow a strategy that works for the client. There are several tools that we use to develop a comprehensive financial plan, including a lifetime cash flow.

Developing the right strategy must start from understanding the individual. Financial services are often 'back to front'. People purchase financial products without having a clear strategy. It's a bit like buying the bricks for a new house without an architect designing it first!

Implementing a client-centric plan

The majority of our time at Provest is spent on understanding the client and developing their plan with them. We address their number one issue before other concerns and provide them with step-by-step, date-driven actions to implement. The deep level of trust we're able to develop with clients by discussing their most important life goals means that whilst their initial concern may, for example, have been pensions, we're able to encourage them to see the 'bigger picture' when it comes to their finances. As a result, we can often build in further aspects of their finances into a plan such as mortgages, savings, investments and estate planning to provide a more complete service.

In addition to understanding their current position, clients can also start to appreciate the financial consequences of likely scenarios or catastrophes. This encourages peace of mind and facilitates crucial decision-making.

Reviewing a client's position

Life is a journey. An elderly parent may pass away. Children or grandchildren arrive, whilst businesses are bought and sold. Life doesn't stand still for anyone, so we need to understand what is happening in our clients' lives to be able to understand their changing priorities, advise them effectively and adjust their financial plans accordingly. External factors such as any stock market crashes and inflation assumptions are considered too. All financial objectives are, therefore, reviewed regularly to check whether clients are still on target.

One of our valued clients was a successful business owner who found himself in debt and stressed out. He was spending too much money and had a house in Florida that he rarely went to. As well as hiring us, he had an accountant and business adviser that he trusted. As his business should have been a vehicle for getting what he wanted out of life, I suggested that we hold joint meetings as his personal advisory board and he later dubbed us his 'dream team'.

Together, we assisted him in making some huge decisions in his personal and business life which helped him tremendously, including reducing his debt, selling his house in Florida and dismissing staff that were no longer productive within his business. For the first time ever, he started saving money and admitted that it wouldn't all have happened without taking the time to stand back and fully understand the bigger picture. Ultimately, he now has clarity and peace of mind.

The value for us and the client lies in the conversations we have with them before going through the financial planning process. Whatever their goals, whether it's achieving financial independence or protecting what they have today, we aim to help our clients achieve what is most important to them.

We can't tell our clients to change their views on money but sometimes they do, when they consider what actually matters to them and what regrets they may have if they don't do what they want, whether that's travelling or spending time with those they care about.

Opening up choices

We all need to understand what choices we can comfortably make. One of our clients was approaching 60 and was increasingly fed up of her stressful job in probation. She was interested in pursuing an alternative part-time job. We determined that this was possible, not in five years' time but right now. We produced a cash-flow model to demonstrate that her expenditure could be maintained if she accepted a part-time role. Of course, choosing to take action was completely her decision but the fact is she knew it was her choice to make.

The right philosophy for creating clients

Given our client-centric way of working, it's hardly surprising that we've achieved some great business benefits. Being client centric has created more clients for us. Our biggest source of new business is 'word of mouth' marketing, generated from existing clients who recommend us to others. This is primarily how our business has grown to date.

The trust that we develop with clients through effective relationship building means that they remain loyal to us and we're able to work closely alongside them to periodically review their finances. Often, clients come to us with a specific concern such as their pension. However, by developing a trusting relationship and encouraging them to think through life goals, there are opportunities for us to develop comprehensive financial plans that focus on many aspects of a client's finances.

We pride ourselves on being problem solvers for clients and I still get a real buzz out of knowing that their lives have improved as a result of our service. I enjoy facilitating extremely important decisions that lead to a better quality of life, such as helping clients to discover they can leave that job they hate or that they can provide for their family in the way they wish to.

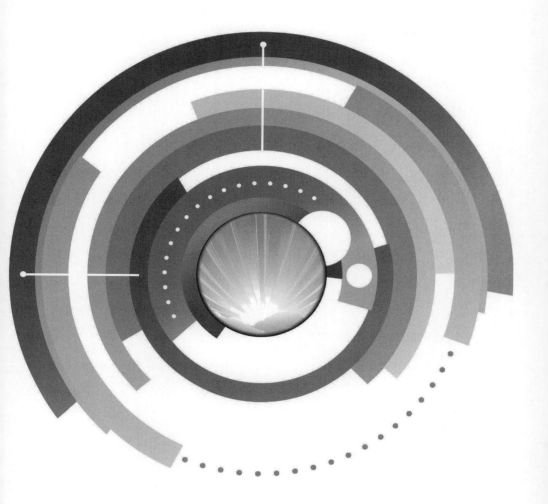

Section 4

New client engagement

In this section we will explore filling your practice with clients who are a joy to serve. This will be a journey through how client acquisition is an inner game, rather than simply a process. When we see and appreciate the true nature of opportunity, where it resides and how best to respond to it, then building your practice becomes fun rather than the chore that so many practitioners seem to experience it as.

Chapter 17

Stop pushing and start connecting

Chapter 17 – Stop pushing and start connecting

Since clients are often anxious and uncertain, they are, above all, looking for someone who will provide reassurance, calm their fears, and inspire confidence.
The Trusted Advisor

I read about the computer company IBM once conducting some research on sales people, which was not specific to financial services but it still makes an important point. They found that:

- 80 per cent of sales people are 'product pushers'
- 15 per cent of sales people are 'solution sellers'
- 5 per cent of sales people are 'trusted advisors' (Raia, 2014)

Why do people push products?

If we look beyond the behaviour of product pushers to what is actually driving it you will see that it is their state of mind. Product pushers are usually that way because they are often, unknowingly, caught up in insecure thinking. For example, they may be creating internal pressure about winning the business, be concerned about how they are coming across or with how things seem to be going.

From a feeling of internal insecurity their attention will turn inwards and towards primarily attending to their own perceived needs, running their own agenda and making a sale, rather than being fully present and putting all their attention on the client and finding out what is really important to them. The product pusher is looking for a situation to sell a product and would often see it as a risk to come off this track and have a much more open conversation because doing so is seen as a potential threat to *their desired* outcome.

Product pushing, by its very nature, is focusing on the completion of a transaction and the relationship will, therefore, be created on the level of supplier and customer.

As we saw in Chapter 1, it is important to realise that money is a means to an end and not the end itself. Therefore, focusing primarily on financial products is focusing upon the means to the end and without exploring what those ends are and what they mean to your client, the opportunity to engage people more deeply is lost.

Solution selling

With solution selling the practitioner's objective is to find a problem that the client is facing now or will face in the future and then solve it. This is often a reactive way of operating and yet it seems to make sense to a lot of advisers.

Of course, financial situations can be complex and there are many circumstances where expert financial advice will be useful to people, but what can often happen is that the adviser is prematurely jumping in to solve the problem and give advice without fully understanding the bigger picture.

As well as turning the relationship into a transactional one, this will often leave an enormous amount of untapped potential for both the client and the adviser, whereas if the adviser were to slow down and be willing to have level three conversations, which we explored in Chapter 7, much more of this potential would be likely to emerge.

As an example, I had several conversations with practitioners about workplace pensions, where they were approaching employers about setting up an arrangement but finding there was very little interest. Even where there was an interest the organisations only wanted to do the very bare minimum.

None of the practitioners I spoke with were having conversations with employers about what might really matter to them, such as how to create higher employee engagement, goodwill or loyalty; the very kind of issue that employers might be highly interested in and see genuine value in. By going in on the back of workplace pensions, and finding little positive response, there was nowhere left to go with the conversation.

Becoming a trusted adviser

Being a trusted adviser is a very special relationship and it is much more than simply gaining trust. It happens when someone holds you in the absolute highest regard and sees you as integral to the creation and fulfilment of their plans. By initially focusing too much on products and financial problems many practitioners are inadvertently lowering the degree of trust and respect they get from clients.

In the book *The Trusted Advisor* by Maister, Green and Galford (2002) it says 'There is no greater source of distrust than advisors who appear to be more interested in themselves than in trying to be of service to the client.'

The book goes on to make the very valid point that self-focus is much more than it just being about being in it for the money. Any form of self-focus, including talking too much about products, investments and financial problems falls into this category too.

Letting go of your outcome

The distinction between a 'product pusher', 'solution seller' and a 'trusted adviser' is a critical element in the process of engaging new clients, because there is a particular state of mind behind each of these that will massively impact the sense of trust that is being communicated.

When we have a high level of psychological functioning (see Chapter 1) we naturally have a low self-orientation and are available to fully focus upon serving the client, which we cannot do if we have some kind of hidden agenda.

If you reflect on the conversations that you conduct with prospective clients, what do you think people would say about you?

Would they say you are deeply curious and interested in them?

Would they say that you are an exceptional listener?

Would they say that you put a great deal into truly understanding who they are and what they want from life before you move on to financial matters?

My experience is that, no matter how good we think we are, we all have significant room for improvement. The biggest single factor in facilitating this improvement is state-of-mind improvement, not skills improvement.

Steve's story

Steve is a highly-qualified financial planner who made the journey, over time, from product selling, through solution selling and ultimately, to being a trusted adviser. Although it may seem like a behavioural change, the real shift in Steve was who he was being, rather than simply what he was doing.

Steve started out his career as a tied agent, providing the products of one company before going independent. His initial training was all about product selling and although he was successful he often felt anxious about where his business was going to come from. He also felt that his client relationships were very transactional, which was not particularly fulfilling for him or them.

As time passed Steve took more qualifications, became more knowledgeable and focused on problem solving and solution selling. The situations he looked for became more complex and involved, which helped him build a bigger income and asset base. However, anxieties remained and he still felt there was more potential to create deeper bonds with his clients.

When I first met Steve his desired outcome was to work with fewer clients of a higher calibre and eliminate the stress he experienced about his business. To Steve, it had always looked as though the stress he suffered was to do with his circumstances. For example, if he was going through a leaner period in his business this used to bring up a lot of insecure thinking and he would have low moods that lasted for days. At these times he would lose his effectiveness and he would often feel tense in meetings with potential clients because he was worried about how the meeting was going to turn out. This could give people a sense of unease and would, at times, result in people not engaging his services. Another product of his insecure thinking was that although he wanted to work with fewer clients he kept taking on clients that did not fit his ideal criteria.

The thought feeling connection

It was extremely helpful for Steve to begin to understand that feelings only come from one place, which is from our thought in the moment, rather than our circumstances.

I shared how, through the great coaching I had received, that I had come to realise that if we think that our sense of wellbeing is dependent upon our circumstances then our experience of life is going to be an emotional roller coaster. When we see the neutrality of the external world then we instinctively return to our sense of wellbeing because we see that it is not dependent on how things go or turn out.

Once his anxious thoughts about the future had become more visible to him Steve realised that he did not need to react to them. When he went to see new potential clients he found that he was far more present, curious and willing to listen. Consequently, his relationships were warmer and people really opened up to him. Over time, his conversion rate of meetings held to new clients engaged went up significantly and he also felt secure enough to engage only the clients he really wanted to work with.

Thoughts to reflect on

Potential clients will feel whether your intention is primarily to sell a product, solve a problem or do whatever it takes to truly understand them and build exceptional trust.

If you reflect on the conversations that you conduct with prospective clients, what do you think people would say about you?

Any form of insecurity, tension or anxiousness, if you see it as 'outside-in', will work against you.

Seeing the thought–feeling connection brings you back to your clarity of mind.

Chapter 18

The source of all opportunity

Chapter 18 – The source of all opportunity

Opportunities? They are all around us. There is power lying latent everywhere waiting for the observant eye to discover it. **Orison Swett Marden**

Opportunity is the lifeblood of growing your practice and in this chapter we will explore how you can instantly open yourself up to seeing far more opportunity and taking effective action to follow through on what you see.

During the 'creating clients' workshops I have run for practitioners I introduce the fact that it is our state of mind that determines the degree to which we are able to see and embrace opportunity in the world. Quite simply, when we are in a clear and present state of mind we are excellent at seeing opportunity and innately know what to do about it. The complete opposite is true when we are consumed by fears, worries and anxieties. In low states of mind we are far too self-consumed to have insightful, creative thinking and much more likely to miss potential opportunities, even when they are right in front of us.

Opportunity is everywhere

I love hearing stories about how people have seen opportunity at the most unlikely times or in the most unlikely of places and if you reflect, I am sure you will notice many times when you have had ideas seemingly out of nowhere. Opportunity is always going to arrive as a thought. Something occurs to you that comes out of the blue. It may be someone to call, an idea about how you can help someone or perhaps something you would like to do. This is your innate wisdom showing up and the more you act upon this kind of thinking, the more generative your thinking becomes.

Martin's story

Back in the early 1990s when I began my career as an adviser I was fortunate enough to see the perfect example of how much difference state of mind makes. In our branch office there were about 40 self-employed advisers and the production figures for the week and the year were on two big whiteboards for everyone to see. There was one adviser, Martin, who consistently and significantly out-performed everyone else and he perfectly demonstrated how to see opportunity where other people saw nothing.

In the office there was a grey metal cupboard full of index cards with details of people who had purchased policies from the company. The company called these people orphan clients because their original adviser had left the company. Some of the cards were years old and yet Martin would take a bunch of them and create business. He would call these people up and talk to them. Everyone else just walked by this cupboard every day without giving it a second glance.

What I saw was that Martin thought differently from everyone else. Where most people saw obstacles, or didn't see anything at all, he saw opportunity. The metal cupboard was just one example, but there were many others. We got to know each other and what I could see was that he was:

- Curious
- Open-minded
- Interested in serving people
- Creative in his approach
- Not affected by people saying they were not interested

He had somehow figured out in his own mind how to stay in his mental clarity and because of this he always had a flow of ideas and he acted upon many of them. He had ups and downs just as we all do but he was extremely resilient and back on track very quickly.

The key to seeing more opportunity

I remember being told about a survey conducted with CEOs of global companies and one of the questions they were asked was 'When do you get your best ideas?' The top three answers were when having a shower, on the drive to or from work and when on holiday. The reason that fresh ideas came to the CEOs at these times was because these were the times when they allowed their minds to relax.

At what times do you tend to get your best ideas?

What difference would it make to you if you had an insightful state of mind far more of the time?

We all have times when we allow our minds to relax and these can seem to be circumstance dependent, just as with the CEOs. However, we have the potential to experience an insightful state of mind far more of the time. The key to this is seeing the inside-out nature of life because the less we have on our minds the more expansive our thinking becomes, which is right at the heart of how well we see opportunity.

What often closes people off from seeing opportunity are feelings of uncertainty and insecurity. For example, if you look out into the future and you cannot see where your next piece of business is coming from or as much money coming in as you want, then how do you react to this? Do you see it as a problem or do you see it as an opportunity? Do you start to get anxious and worry or do you feel relaxed?

Many of us have taken on this idea that we have to worry or punish ourselves into better performance. But if we scare ourselves with our own thinking then it lowers our state of mind, we become bereft of ideas and it constricts our view of the world, including our ability to see and effectively act upon opportunity. Psychologist and author of *Emotional Intelligence: Why it can matter more than IQ* (1996), Daniel Goleman insightfully said 'Our worries become self-fulfilling prophecies, propelling us toward the very disaster they predict.'

Other people's ideas are great... for them!

If it seems that we have no ideas of our own then this is when we are most likely to grasp for someone else's ideas, like a drowning person holding onto a lifebelt. I have attended many workshops and seminars on sales and marketing over the years and would often find that my enthusiasm would go up immediately after an event but then wane. Sometimes the ideas I got did help but they never seemed to be the complete answer.

It wasn't until I began to really understand the role of thought that I realised why I kept feeling the need to try to get ideas from other people. What I have found infinitely more useful, both for myself and my clients, is knowing that we have access to an unlimited number of ideas of our own and that, when we allow our minds to relax we will always get high-quality, productive thinking. I might still find other people's ideas interesting and occasionally helpful but they will never be as good as my own because our own insights are perfectly tailored to us as well as being the ones we tend to get behind the most.

The secret to more opportunity

We are most open to new thinking when we feel calm, relaxed and free from internal pressure. If we keep looking to the outside world for our source of ideas or salvation we are looking in totally the wrong direction and it tends to perpetuate feelings of insecurity. Seeing the thought/feeling connection returns us to a sense of ease and confident self-reliance, which is our foundation for generative thinking and the secret to more opportunity.

So, if you ever feel that you do not have enough opportunity in front of you then it is useful to reflect upon the following question:

What would happen if I had a completely clear mind?

This question will often clear the way for new thinking because we realise that seeing opportunity is state-of-mind dependent. By taking the pressure off ourselves and relaxing, our thinking becomes of a far higher quality and more expansive.

Thoughts to reflect on

Opportunities are everywhere, all of the time.

Feeling insecure and uncertain is what prevents us from seeing opportunity.

Mental clarity is the key to seeing more opportunity and knowing innately what to do about it.

The more you act upon your insights the more generative your thinking becomes.

Chapter 19

The very best marketing you can do

Chapter 19 – The very best marketing you can do

Effective engagement is inspired by the empathy that develops simply by being human.
Brian Solis

One of the challenges for the financial professional when speaking to a potential client is engaging the client in such a way that they really experience what financial planning can do for them rather than simply hearing about it as a concept.

The fact is that money is an emotional subject for many people. Talking about how we want to live our lives, our desires, our dreams, our hopes and our fears is emotional. As we saw in Chapter 7 on the three levels of client conversation, logic may make people think but it is emotion that makes people act. A conceptual approach means talking about financial planning as a technical, linear, step-by-step, numbers-based process, which is taking an intellectual approach to an emotional subject.

The consequence of talking about financial planning as a concept is that it takes people into logical, analytical thinking, which is asking them to do mental work. So, instead of having mental clarity, which is how good decisions are made, it will cause some people to feel confused, insecure or uncertain. Inadvertently, if a practitioner keeps the conversation on a logical/analytical level it can create a trust issue because the client and what matters most to them is not being put right at the very centre.

Chris's story

Chris is a chartered financial planner who prided himself on his academic ability and his approach to his work was very analytical. The problem he created for himself was that he mistakenly thought that because he valued this quality so highly in himself, his clients also would. It was true that some of them did appreciate this approach but many times people had difficulty in really connecting with Chris. They found him aloof and sometimes difficult to engage with.

What Chris could not see was the amount of thinking he was doing and how this was negatively affecting the tone of his meetings. For example, Chris would talk to prospective clients about their financial situations and start to jump in where he saw something he thought he could help with. He would talk about financial planning in a very conceptual way and start to get technical and explain how he could help them deal with the issues he saw.

Chris thought that very high-quality advice, technically speaking, was what clients wanted and he put all his energy into this. He could not understand why he seemed to get so much resistance from people. Some would put him off, some would take ages to make a decision and some went elsewhere.

Most people initially do not know what financial planning is. How often have you had someone banging on your door saying 'Please, I need you to create me a financial plan immediately!'? It does not really happen like this and therefore, it is up to you to create an environment that has someone feeling compelled to engage you.

Underneath Chris's approach was his own insecure thinking, which was why he felt he needed to prove himself. His idea of the best way to do this was by showing his expertise in financial matters, but this often worked against him because he was inadvertently making prospective clients feel insecure too.

The client-centred experience

Imagine you own a car dealership. It is easy to give a prospective buyer the keys to a car and say 'Why don't you take this car for a test drive so you can really *feel* what it is like to own it.' Although the buyer's experience is still their thought in the moment, it is a very engaging experience because all the senses are highly involved. Clever car dealerships have used this process to good effect for years, with some manufacturers of luxury cars actually giving prospective customers a car for a whole weekend.

As a financial practitioner you do not have the luxury of having someone engage with and test a tangible product. Therefore, you have to create their experience conversationally, which is not done using your intellectual mind. You have to get deeply, intensely curious because this is what demonstrates your genuine commitment to understanding someone. You want them as involved, right from the very beginning, as much as if they were driving a luxury car.

Let me give you an example. Leading financial planner Andy Jervis at Chesterton House Financial Planning Ltd (who has contributed a guest chapter to this book, see Chapter 13) knows how to create a powerful client experience. Andy has a deep, inner confidence in what he does and he is willing to be present, ask powerful questions and listen at level three. That experience is unusual and very positive for people but Andy goes further. He often gives his clients tasks so that they get involved in the process. If they say they want to go on the trip of a lifetime then Andy will get them to go and do some research and obtain brochures and he holds them accountable. As a result of the conversation with Andy people feel and act differently. Andy does not need to sell a concept. He creates a powerful experience and he is serving his clients right from the very beginning and not simply once they have engaged his services.

Slow down and put in more up front

First and foremost, when speaking with a prospective client you will best serve them and yourself by being present. Many practitioners create problems for themselves, as Chris did, by going too fast, which is driven by their insecure thinking.

When you are willing to slow things right down and put more in up front you have the opportunity to take people beyond a concept and let them really feel what it is like to work with you. The number one priority is that you facilitate your potential clients experiencing mental clarity, healthy psychological functioning and connecting with what is most important to them.

When it comes to the decision of you working together it is not your job to try to 'close' them or become anxious about what happens next. Steve Chandler, an expert in client engagement, says 'Their decision should not be about whether to start. It should be about whether to continue.' When you get people moving towards what is really important to them then they are far more likely to want to continue because it just makes sense.

The magic bullet

It seems to me that many practitioners are looking for the 'magic bullet' of how to get lots of good quality leads and yet they miss the most obvious thing of all, which is giving people a powerful, emotional and memorable experience.

Every second you are with a client is marketing and, as we know, the most effective form of marketing is word of mouth. People tell other people, such as their family, friends and colleagues, about powerful, deeply engaging experiences because this is what they remember. They are highly likely to forget a technical conversation about pensions and very unlikely to have it as a dinner party subject!

The problem in financial services is that the focus for many years has been on improving technical knowledge and gaining qualifications. There seems to be this idea that if you become more and more qualified then clients will be attracted to you. I fully support advisers knowing what they are talking about, but treating financial planning as an intellectual subject gets in the way of many practitioners building a practice as quickly and effectively as they would like.

People do not want intellectual discussions about financial planning. In many cases, getting analytical, intellectual and technical will make clients retreat into their heads and do too much thinking and this gets in the way of them having clarity of mind. This is the absolute reverse of what you want happening.

You want people to have warm, positive feelings. You want them to feel invigorated and inspired. You want them to have expansive and clear thinking. The *only* way this can happen is when you feel this way yourself, which is impossible if you do not have a high level of psychological functioning.

Thoughts to reflect on

To engage new clients most effectively, involve them emotionally and avoid talking conceptually about what financial planning can do.

You can create powerful, emotional experiences conversationally.

Slow down and be willing to put in more up front.

Technical knowledge is important but it is not why people hire you.

Chapter 20

Five steps to your next
client

Chapter 20 – Five steps to your next client

No idea will work if people don't trust your intentions toward them.
Marcus Buckingham

Philip wanted to grow his practice. I recall our very first conversation and while on the surface I could hear him describing how he wanted to bring on more clients, increase funds under management and create a bigger income I could sense there was some stress or tension behind his words.

When we first began working together Philip talked about sales, targets and numbers. Building his practice had become a very impersonal experience for him and I remember asking him 'Do you notice that when you talk about growing your practice you never talk about people, you only talk about processes and numbers?'

This took Philip by surprise and caused him to reflect. He could see that the joy had disappeared from his work. He had got caught up in the trap of 'I'll be happy when...'. His happiness always seemed to be out in the future and dependent upon the attainment of the goals he had set.

This kind of scenario is extremely common amongst business people, including financial services professionals. Leading management thinker and author of *What Got You Here Won't Get You There: How successful people become even more successful*, Marshall Goldsmith (2008) said 'The great western disease is that we fixate on the future at the expense of enjoying the life we're living now.'

Before I learned about state of mind and where it comes from I used to suffer from 'the great western disease'. Tomorrow always used to seem more attractive than today because I thought that I needed my external conditions to be a certain way before I felt OK. This had big implications for building my business because I had created this self-imposed feeling of being under pressure. Although I could not see it at the time this internal pressure caused me to lose my spark because it looked circumstance related.

Philip did not need to be coached on how to bring on new clients. He knew how to do this already but his busy mind and attachment to the future had caused him to lose his spark. Once he began to understand the role of thought he could step away from all that mental activity and allow his wisdom to show up. By relaxing into the present he naturally returned to doing what he came into the business for in the first place; spending time with people whose company he enjoys and making a difference in their lives.

Whatever way you approach engaging new clients there are five steps that are always present. The state of mind that you bring to each step is a far bigger factor in your effectiveness than the details of the process. As you read through each step you can reflect upon your quality of thinking around each step in your own practice and open your mind to insights and new thinking that helps you improve your approach.

Step 1 – Connecting

All client-centred relationships begin by connecting with someone in a human way, which means connecting in such a way that our thinking is not contaminated by our own imaginary needs. When we have clarity of mind we are excellent at connecting with people because we give out the feeling of being at ease with ourselves and people find this attractive and reassuring.

Many practitioners, because they operate from a base of insecure thinking, make connecting on a meaningful level far more difficult than it ever needs to be. For example, if your primary intention is looking for an opening to push a product or to find a financial problem to solve, then this will often create a barrier because it makes people suspicious of your motives. Many clients of financial advisers probably only hear from their adviser when he or she wants to sell them something with this being wrapped up in the disguise of it being time for a 'review'.

Connecting in a human way is about being curious, interested, authentic, transparent and service orientated. There are dozens of ways to connect with people and the secret to building your practice is being open to what your own wisdom sends you, doing what you enjoy and what comes most naturally to you. As an example, for 15 years I have written a digital newsletter that goes out each month. Over the years I have enrolled many clients because they have got in touch through reading my articles, but I write because I enjoy writing and want to provide useful content not because I am only interested in getting a client.

Ask yourself:

- In what ways do I enjoy connecting with and serving people?
- What activities come easily to me?
- What has worked well/is working well now for me?

It could be through meeting people face-to-face, third-party introductions, through writing, speaking, or some kind of affiliation. If you want to connect with people genuinely then put them at the centre and deliver real value. I have known some of my adviser clients put on events where they invite people along, give them something to eat and allow them to network in a friendly and exclusive environment. Some advisers focus on a particular market niche and become a useful resource that people can call upon. Others enjoy building associations with other professionals so they can offer peace of mind for their clients when they need a professional service.

The number one way to connect with someone new is to be highly recommended by someone they listen to and respect. If you take a step back from this, who do you think gets better and more introductions, 'trusted advisers' or 'product pushers'? People will willingly refer you when they trust you and know you will provide a great experience to the person they are referring. If they think you are in it primarily for your own gain then you will not get many introductions.

Ultimately, the best situation to create is to have people coming to you because this creates the dynamic of the relationship in an ideal way. By focusing on giving, in whichever ways you enjoy doing, you begin to create a momentum where more and more people will seek you out.

Step 2 – Inviting someone into a conversation

One of my coaches, Fiona Jacob, shared with me that she always asks herself two questions in relation to engaging potential new clients.

- Can I help?
- Do I want to?

When you are connecting with people on a regular basis then you are going to see situations where you can genuinely help. But this does not necessarily mean that you want to, which is why the second question is important.

One of the keys to working with great clients and having the relationship on the right footing is being clear about what it takes to work with you. A few years ago I remember being curious about working with a particular coach and I said to him 'Shall we have a chat?' He said 'No, I don't have "chats". If you are really interested then let's schedule in two hours together and have a powerful conversation about what you really want to accomplish in life.'

This immediately set the tone. He was leaving the door wide open for me to walk away and, at the same time, letting me know who I needed to be to get involved.

My own approach is different but nevertheless my intention is that when I invite someone into a conversation I want to set the right tone. I have found that by doing this you will ultimately engage better clients as the ones who are likely to waste your time tend to fall at the first hurdle because they are not committed.

Inviting someone into a conversation is easy when you have nothing riding on the outcome. It is as simple as innocently asking 'Would you like to talk about this?' or 'Do you want to set up a conversation to explore this further?' or 'I may be able to help here, do you want to talk?'

A barrier that some practitioners create for themselves is that they have a lot of insecure thinking about making invitations and requests because they fear being turned down. Being afraid of rejection is entirely a state-of-mind issue and has nothing to do with the response to a request. We have all had the experience of hearing the word 'no' and feeling bad about it, just as we have all had the experience of hearing the word 'no' and it having no effect at all or even feeling good about it.

If we feel tense or under pressure then it can only be our thinking in the moment that is causing us to feel this way and as soon as we see this then we will stop being so gripped by our thinking. The fact is that if you are participating in life, doing what you do, then people will turn you down. When we understand that this is inevitable and it has no meaning whatsoever then we can ask for whatever we want because the response does not matter.

Step 3 – Conversations

If someone has expressed an interest or you see that you may be able to help them and you have invited them into a conversation, then what kind of conversation will you have? Will it be one where you tell them all about you, your company and the service you can provide? Will it be one where you talk about the possibility of working together?

This is what many advisers do, but there is huge potential to go beyond the limitation of this kind of conversation and serve people more deeply, right from the very first contact.

There is a term used in marketing called the 'horoscope effect' and what this means is that if someone is into horoscopes and they turn to that section of a publication, then where are they most likely to look first? Almost certainly their own sign, of course. So, if they are an Aries they are unlikely to look at Virgo first. Why would they because it has got nothing to do with them?

Telling someone all about you, your company and your service is the equivalent of telling them about somebody else's star sign. Why would they be interested in that? They are not interested in you talking about how long you have been in business, how many qualifications you have or how great you are. I do appreciate that there is a requirement to provide certain information to potential clients but this can be done at the appropriate time.

An example, and one I have used many times, is setting the tone of a conversation immediately by asking a question like 'What will make this meeting a brilliant use of your time?' This question is entirely in the world of your client. Nothing is more powerful than putting someone right at the centre and engaging them in a level three conversation (see Chapter 7). This will take care of their questions about whether they can trust you and you know what you are talking about because it is all about them.

Step 4 – Proposals

When you have conversations that are powerful enough then some people will ask you directly 'So, how do we work together?' For them it is about continuing and not starting, so if you do want to make a proposal (and sometimes you won't) then you can go ahead and do so in whatever way makes sense to you.

In cases where you have a conversation and the person has not yet asked how they can work with you then allow your intuition to guide you. There is no one approach that is 'right'. Sometimes you may ask the question 'What do you want to do next?' or 'What do you feel comfortable doing next?' There will be other times where people want stronger leadership from you and it will be of service to them for you to take the lead and direct the process.

There is a lot of sales training advice that tells you that you must control the situation. However, any form of trying to impose your will upon someone will create resistance because it gives people something to push back against. People feel where you are coming from and if they suspect you are working any form of your own agenda then it will work against you. The need to control is driven by insecurity. At all stages of your client relationships, when you are completely client centred, there is nothing for people to push back against.

Step 5 – Continue... or not

Exactly the same as at the proposal stage, nothing is more important than being in your clarity of mind and open to your own wisdom in each situation.

Engaging your services will be a significant decision for potential clients and some of them will have insecure thinking about making the commitment. Some will say 'yes' immediately, some will want to think about it and, occasionally, some may decide not to go ahead. That is business and is inevitable. By staying in a clear mind you can respond intuitively to a situation rather than from neediness.

For example, if you chase a prospective client for a decision about going ahead from a feeling of insecurity, then it will not only change the dynamic of the relationship to a less useful one, it could also negatively influence someone's decision to work with you. However, if you follow someone up when you have in a clear mind they will experience you as you being helpful and service orientated.

Thoughts to reflect on

All client acquisition involves connecting, inviting, conversations, proposals and continuing (or not).

Connecting with people is effortless and natural when you are in a clear state of mind.

Before inviting someone into a conversation, ask yourself 'Can I help?' and 'Do I want to?'

The most powerful conversations are client-centred conversations, not adviser-centred conversations.

Allow your clarity of mind and intuition to guide you at the proposal stage and beyond.

Chapter 21

Too much information

Chapter 21 – Too much information

Why is it that with all the information available today on how to be successful in small business, so few people really are? **Michael Gerber**

David's story

David is an established financial planner whose practice had for several years hit a plateau, achieving approximately the same turnover for four consecutive years. David wanted to expand the practice and yet it just was not happening for him.

The practice certainly had the capacity to handle an increased workload and it would have been very easy to conclude that the root of the problem was the lack of marketing. It was true that the practice was doing very little to generate new business and had been relying on existing clients, so surely the creation and execution of a marketing plan would solve the problem and start to bring in business?

The situation was that David had regularly heard this advice many times at professional events. He had even had a consultant in to address the issue, who had accurately noted the lack of action taking place and recommended a number of practical steps. But David just did not seem to engage with the advice he was getting.

I had a couple of conversations with David and I wanted to understand how he saw things. It seemed that, on one level, he wanted to build his business but I was also curious to find out what he thought was stopping him. He had a few different answers to this, ranging from not knowing what to do through to lacking discipline and motivation. I also noted how critical David was of himself.

The busy mind

At the root of the situation was that David has a busy mind, which is extremely common and something that has become an unconscious habit for many people. We can get this idea that we need to think our way through life and, therefore, are always occupying our minds. Consequently, it begins to look as if the busy mind is the symptom of a busy life when, in fact, it is completely the other way around.

Too much information

When we begin to overthink things we often end up taking no action at all or are ineffective in what we do. An overly busy mind is a major contributory factor to many people's poor performance because they often have no clear sense of direction. After all, if you have hundreds of thoughts whizzing around inside your mind then which ones do you pay attention to?

From a state of confusion it can often look as if what is missing is information because if we had the answer already then surely it would be obvious, wouldn't it? So we can end up becoming information junkies, always looking for that missing piece that will set us on our way.

The ultimate solution is always a better state of mind

If we feel confused, uncertain or lack clarity about what to do then it is a sure sign that our thinking is of low quality. In these kinds of state we are never going to get useful, clear thinking that we really get behind and take action. By seeing that our experience is coming from thought in the moment, the only place it can ever come from, our mind begins to quieten down and we reconnect to our resourcefulness.

David did not need more information or any more helpful advice about what to do. What really helped him was a deeper understanding of state of mind and what creates it. He reflected and said, 'I just did not consider how my thinking was creating the confusion I was experiencing. I kept berating myself for being stuck and was just making the situation even worse! Once I could see that I was stirring up my own mind I just seemed to naturally stop because it made no sense to keep thinking into everything.'

Over the next 12 months David's practice began to grow healthily. Instead of living up in his head so much of the time he developed an appreciation of having an insightful state of mind and as a result he relaxed and began to have clear, useful thoughts that he acted upon. He created a plan that was based around what he enjoyed doing and so, in its execution, it felt effortless. David also stopped being so harsh and critical with himself because he realised that he was driving down his state of mind by doing so and actually lowering his performance.

If you think that what is holding you back is a lack of information then it is useful to reflect upon your state of mind. I have found that a lack of information is rarely, if ever, what holds people back. It just appears that way.

When you feel stuck then simply turn your attention to your feeling state and ask yourself 'Where is my feeling coming from? Is it coming from my circumstances or is it coming from my thought in the moment?' As soon as we see it is our thought in the moment, the only place it can ever be, it reorientates us back to the present and high-quality thinking.

Thoughts to reflect on

When you feel 'stuck' it is an indicator of your quality of mind not a lack of information.

The need for more and more information is usually a product of busy, confused thinking.

Seeing the thought/feeling connection is what clears our mind.

With a clear mind we always know what to do.

Chapter 22

The fee conversation

Chapter 22 – The fee conversation

Fees are part and parcel of your overall strategic approach to your market. They should never constitute your single driving force, nor should they be dictated by the client or competition. **Alan Weiss**

In the process of engaging a new client the fee conversation will have to take place at some point and what primarily causes practitioners problems in the area of fees is insecure thinking. This is not only in the process of making a proposal but also much earlier, in the process of actually arriving at fee levels in the first place.

It seems to me that many practitioners and firms arrive at their fees by looking at what other practitioners are charging. Some then charge less believing that they are offering a 'good deal' to clients. Some charge more because they think they are offering a premium service. Some charge the same because it seems to be the going rate.

However, comparing yourself to others, in whatever way you do it, is commoditising what you do. Instead of thinking of yourself as similar it is far more effective to emphasise your uniqueness, which you can only do when you feel secure and comfortable with who you are and the value that you create for people.

What are you charging for?

The problem that many practitioners and firms create for themselves is completely misunderstanding what they can actually charge for. The vast majority of the profession thinks it is charging for services and by doing this it is reducing what they do to the status of a commodity and inviting comparison. For example, by working on the level of providing products or solving financial problems then it is unavoidably offering a service which, no matter how good, can only attract a certain fee.

Creating transformation

What is way beyond a comparable service is genuine transformation, which you can measure by asking yourself the question 'How much difference am I really making?'

Arranging financial products for a client is helpful. Solving a financial problem is helpful. But neither of these is likely to create a truly transformational experience for your client. However, when you confidently know that you can enter someone's life and through your conversations with them and the subsequent work you do, have them thinking and acting differently and so experiencing both immediate and lasting emotionally felt benefit, then this is transformational.

When your client's most important life goals become more alive and real for them they will feel inspired and motivated to follow through with actions that count, creating a virtuous circle. When they experience their valued states of mind such as more peace of mind, freedom, joy, security, safety, integrity, less worry and a greater feeling of wellbeing, this will be worth a great deal to them. This is when your strong fees are seen as a highly worthwhile investment for which they pay willingly.

To create a transformational experience the onus on you, as the practitioner, is to:

- Fully engage your clients and identify what they really want from life.
- Identify what could stop them.
- Create a plan that clearly gets them where they want to go.
- Hold them accountable to what they need to do.
- Teach or coach them, where appropriate.
- Bring them back on track when they falter.

What to charge?

What is most important is to follow your inner guidance on what to charge. What people will hear and feel when you state your fees is where you are coming from. If you are full of insecurity, uncertainty and fear then this will leak out like a sieve and cause problems. You will stammer, stutter and avert your eyes, which gives the game away that you feel uncomfortable.

When your thinking is congruent with what you charge then it will be no different to giving out your phone number. It is just factual information.

The analytical approach to fees

Knowing what you need to charge to run your business and make a reasonable profit is responsible trading because undercharging and going out of business does not help anyone. Therefore, taking an analytical approach to calculating your fees provides a scientifically based number compared to one picked at random. However, such a number must still be communicated to clients cogently to avoid problems.

Julie's story

Julie is a financial planner who used to have a lot of insecure thinking about her fees and, as happens to every professional person, a client occasionally queried her fees and what they were getting for their money.

Many people have insecure thinking around money and so, inevitably, some will baulk at your fees. The problem is never a client's reaction to your fees; it is your reaction to their reaction. If someone feels insecure about your fees and this, in turn, provokes an insecure reaction from you it invites problems. Two people feeling insecure does not create a healthy situation.

I asked Julie whether she thought her fees provided genuine value and she said that they did. So, the real issue was not her fees but her reaction to being questioned about her fees. She could see that if someone queried her fees she would get defensive and she was inadvertently inviting even more pushback from clients.

Once she could see what was going on she realised that she did not need to respond from her own insecure thinking. Just because a client started to feel insecure about her fees she could see that reacting to this was like throwing petrol on the flames.

Sometime after our conversation about fees Julie reported back to me on a situation with a prospective client who had questioned her fee. The client had said 'This seems a lot of money?' Instead of getting defensive, Julie had remained in her clarity of mind and simply said 'Yes, it is a significant amount.' She said the client sat back, thought for a moment and then visibly lightened up as he said 'Let's go ahead, I've been wanting to do this for ages.'

This does not mean to say that every person you offer a proposal to will say 'yes'. Some will not, but the only thing that could make this a problem is if you attach your sense of wellbeing to getting a 'yes'. I have worked with practitioners who do not take getting turned down well and it weighs on them, which clearly serves no useful purpose. By understanding the inside-out nature of life, even if we have an initial negative reaction to something, we quickly return to a sense of ease and clarity because we realise that the situation was neutral and our feeling can only be coming from our thought in the moment about the situation. This takes us out of destructive win/lose thinking.

A potential client accepted a significant proposal to work together and a few days later I went on holiday. Whilst away I received an email from the client saying he had changed his mind. Initially, I was a little perplexed but I decided to forget about it and only respond when I returned. Once I got back I contacted the client and suggested we speak and it turned out that some well-meaning 'friends' of the client had been giving their opinions and he had started to doubt his decision. I recentred the client on his ultimate outcome, addressed the doubts and he went ahead. This wouldn't have happened if I had taken it personally and lost my ability to think clearly.

Increasing your fees

You may have existing clients on a certain fee level and want to increase it. Once again, your state of mind is right at the centre. If you are losing money on a client then why would you continue with them? You will go out of business if you do too much of this. Also, if you are doing too much for what you are being paid then this is equally bad. You cannot run a viable, long-term business in this way.

What feeling insecure does is fool practitioners into short-term thinking and so it has them grabbing what they can. When you think long term, from a clear and secure state of mind, you will not feel inclined to take on unprofitable work or work you do not want to do.

Ultimately, people pay for what they consider good value. If you want to charge higher fees then make a bigger difference in the lives of your clients. Care for them deeply, focus on what matters most to them and enhance their lives. People are willing to pay well to get what they really want in life.

Thoughts to reflect on

It is only the practitioner's insecure thinking that causes problems in the area of fees.

Are you charging for products, a service or genuine transformation?

Genuine transformation is what clients are willing to pay strong fees for.

To increase your fees, increase your clients' perception of your value.

Chapter 23

Ditch the pitch

Chapter 23 – Ditch the pitch

The privilege of a lifetime is being who you are. **Joseph Campbell**

If someone is going to engage your services in such an important area as entrusting you with their financial wellbeing then, of course, they will want to feel entirely confident that you know what you are doing. Also, they want to deal with someone they feel is honest and who will act with integrity and transparency. The question is 'How is this best communicated?'

I have had some practitioners tell me that when meeting a new potential client they give some kind of pitch. Usually, this is a version of 'Let me tell you about me and my company' and they talk about their experience, their qualifications, how long they have been in business and what they can do (exactly what most websites do, by the way).

The intention may be to reassure the person but, in reality, this is making it about you and it is not about you; it is about the client. I call this kind of self-focused behaviour 'focusing inwards' because it is trying to prove credibility through telling rather than demonstrating it by putting the client right at the centre.

Although I am sure that people who take this approach do not see it like this, it is like being the bore you meet at a party who does nothing but talk about themselves. It betrays insecurity on the part of the practitioner because it's about trying to control the situation.

There may well be a time and place to share information about your business and yourself but using this as an opening 'pitch' is usually a mistake. You cannot go wrong when your focus of attention is completely upon who you are with rather than how you are coming across.

What about if someone asks you 'What do you do?'

There are likely to be times when someone asks you 'What do you do?', for example, at a networking function. It seems that there is a whole legion of 'experts' who advise that you should have a pre-prepared and rehearsed answer to this question in the form of a pitch (sometimes known as an 'elevator pitch').

The idea of an 'elevator pitch' is that you can deliver it in the short time it takes to go up in a lift. Your pitch is supposed to be clever, engaging and pre-rehearsed so that when you deliver it, it will be smooth and polished.

Of course, the idea of creating a clever, engaging and pre-rehearsed way of describing what you do seems very convincing as I am sure we all want to create a good impression when we meet someone for the first time. We all want to convey what we do in a way that people find compelling and avoid being dull, boring and forgettable! Despite all this making sense, in trying to create one for myself the problem I had was not only describing what I did in a few sentences; it was also making it sound like me.

The thing with pitching, in any form, is that it will often come across as unnatural, because it is! The original idea of the 'elevator pitch' came from the tech world. The story goes that if you were a young tech entrepreneur and you happened to get into a lift with Bill Gates and he said 'What do you do?' (as I am sure he regularly does!), you have between 30 seconds and two minutes to pitch him your idea for seed capital for your business, so it had better be good.

This idea has somehow got out into the mainstream business world, but imagine going to a networking function where you are potentially going to meet lots of new people. Does it really make sense to deliver the same thing over and over again? If you met 15 people would you want to say the same thing 15 times over? And does doing this actually work?

What do people really buy into?

I attended breakfast networking groups for over ten years and heard literally thousands of pitches because each participant (and there could be up to 40 people at each meeting) had 30 seconds to deliver their pitch. I heard funny ones, brilliant ones and some appallingly bad ones, but what was far more important to me was not the words, it was who was behind the words.

I remember success coach Michael Neill telling a story about a guy he knows who won the world elevator speech championships (yes, apparently there is even a world championship for this!). During a conversation they had Michael asked him how much business his wonderful elevator pitch had won him. His reply was that he had never, ever had one single piece of business from it. He said he had business from being the elevator pitch champion but not directly from the pitch itself.

Financial planning is a business based upon the very highest levels of trust and integrity and practitioners are not young tech entrepreneurs looking for an investor. Just blindly pitching at someone will more than likely work against you rather than for you because people see through it.

The power is not in the words

What people want is for you to be authentic. They want to connect with you in a human way and the only way this can happen is if you are present and unattached to the outcome.

A successful businesswoman I know recently sat on a panel at a business conference. The subject was 'practice building' and a question from someone in the audience was 'What is the best way to approach describing your business if someone asks you "What do you do?"' Her reply was that she just says what occurs to her at the time. She explained that every situation and every person is different, therefore, it makes no sense to her to trot out the same line over and over.

This does not mean to say that you should not have compelling ways to describe what you do or have some useful stories to tell because at the right time this can be powerful.

It means that when you are present (i.e. not focusing inwards) you will know how best to respond in that particular moment.

What people feel is where you are coming from. They feel your state of mind. Just robotically pitching at people is when we have switched off, gone onto autopilot and given up the opportunity to really connect.

Be who you are

One of the most watched TED talks is Simon Sinek's 'How great leaders inspire action', with around 20 million views. The core message of this talk is 'People don't buy what you do; they buy why you do it'. Telling people what you do is information. Sharing why you do it comes from your heart and this is what people feel.

We have a choice in life. We can be some version of ourselves that we think the world wants to see or that some 'expert' has told us we need to be. This is what you might call the conditioned self, the commercial personality or the attraction package, which is what the idea of the elevator pitch is. Our other choice is to let our real authentic selves shine through. This is effortless because you do not have to try to be who you really are and this is what people buy into, not some polished, made up version of you.

Thoughts to reflect on

Trying to prove your credibility will often work against you.

What people buy into is where you are coming from and not just what you say or do.

By all means have useful ways to describe what you do but respond in the moment rather than like a robot.

Be who you are; not some made up version of yourself.

Chapter 24

**Being client centred is
not something you do:
it is a state of mind**

Chapter 24 – Being client centred is not something you do: it is a state of mind

The state of your life is nothing more than a reflection of your state of mind.
Wayne Dyer

When you put your client right at the centre it communicates everything that creates an exceptionally high-quality relationship – human connection, trust, caring, understanding and responsiveness.

Your healthy state of mind is by far the most significant factor in enabling you to put your client right at the centre. It is what allows you to step out of your own world and into theirs. Any form of self-focus, self-interest or self-orientation will contaminate the relationship and impair your ability to deeply connect with your client and do transformational work.

A healthy, secure and free state of mind is what we all have when we are not overburdened with unhelpful thinking. When your thinking is clear then it is natural and easy to build high-quality relationships and effectively build your practice.

In the first section of the book we explored how, in today's business environment, being client centred is the most viable, sustainable and high-reward business model. We made the state-of-mind factor visible and, in Chapter 2, we saw that there are very clear and precise scientific principles behind the working of the mind.

These principles are not a technique. You do not 'do' these principles, as some people have mistakenly assumed. The inside-out understanding tells us that our feelings can only ever come from our thought in the moment. This stops us being a victim of circumstances because when your thinking is 'off', and it is for all of us at times, you will know why. Consequently, you can move through your lows more gracefully and return to presence and clarity of mind more quickly.

Who you are being is far more important than what you are doing. Our results emerge from the actions that we take but it is our clarity of mind that determines the quality of our actions. For example, people who are endlessly busy are usually reactive, firefighting and wasting a lot of time because their busy-minded thinking prevents them having the clarity of mind of knowing what to say 'yes' to and what to say 'no' to.

In Section 2 we explored the core elements of building client-centred relationships. All of these elements are a product of a clear state of mind, rather than being techniques. For instance, connecting with people in a human way that communicates a deep sense of trust is a by-product of mental clarity.

It is very easy to overcomplicate financial advice and this can make a subject which, for many people, is already a source of stressful thinking, even more daunting. By having a quiet mind and being fully focused upon your client, you can facilitate a rich, engaging and rewarding experience for them. You know you are on the right track when your clients genuinely find your meetings uplifting, inspiring and of extremely high value.

You do not ever need to allow your insecure thinking to prevent you moving from a transactional-based model to a client-centred model. You cannot really go wrong when transitioning to having deeper conversations with your clients. It may possibly feel uncomfortable for you in the very beginning but when your intention is to genuinely serve your client they will appreciate the depth of interest you are taking in them.

In Section 3 you read contributions from five successful client-centred practitioners. You read that each has their own unique approach to their work and yet they all share the ability to have the client see the bigger picture, rather than simply focusing upon financial products and problems. They all work in the context of the client's life holistically by integrating life goals and money, rather than treating finances as a separate subject. This enables them to build closer, more mutually beneficial relationships that are highly rewarding in many ways.

In Section 4 we looked at the process of engaging new clients. Practice building does take time, effort and commitment but what makes it difficult for practitioners is going about it in unhelpful states of mind, which takes all the fun and enjoyment out of it.

The world is full of opportunities and from a clear mind we easily see and know what to do about them. Real, genuine and lasting inner security does not come from what you have; it comes from knowing that you can create. When we appreciate the potential of the system we live in, we stop looking outside ourselves for answers because we know that we live in a world of infinite possibility and opportunity.

Although there are a lot of so-called 'experts' telling us that we need to present some kind of 'polished' version of ourselves to the world, nothing is better than being who you are.

One problem, one solution

In the external world there could be an infinite number and variety of challenges you might face and, of course, there will always be obstacles to overcome. However, we can either get caught up in unhealthy thinking about them or we can approach them with clear thinking and, therefore, negotiate them as easily as possible.

With greater clarity of mind and psychological freedom our 'improvement curve' just naturally sharpens. Instead of trying to force success and make it happen, it comes to us.

Clarity of mind is all we ever need. With a clear mind, free from negative, unhelpful thinking, we are free to perform at our best. It really is that simple. Most people vastly underestimate just how much difference mental clarity makes. I did and sometimes I still forget, as we all will at times. Our state of mind is so easy to overlook because, as we saw in Chapter 2, we are like fish in water; it looks to us as though we are directly experiencing our circumstances.

Perhaps the greatest gift of the inside-out understanding is that it relieves us of the burden of believing that we have to think our way through life. We have an innate intelligence available to us all the time. This wisdom will guide us through life and the greater the appreciation we have for it, the more effortless, easy and enjoyable life becomes.

What is next for you?

We always have a choice. Our next moment can be a rerun of our old, habitual thinking or it can feel completely fresh. When we live in the present, each moment can be like looking at a breathtaking view for the very first time. Every conversation can be alive and invigorating. Building a client-centred business becomes a joy.

Bibliography

Banks, S. (1998) *The Missing Link: Reflections on philosophy and spirit*. Canada: Lone Pine Publishing

Carlson, R. (1998) *Slowing Down to the Speed of Life: How to create a more peaceful, simpler life from the inside out*. Harper Collins

Chandler, S. (2006) *Joy of Selling*. Robert D. Reed Publishers

Csikszentmihalyi, M. (2002) *Flow: The classic work on how to achieve happiness*. Rider

Gallwey, T. (1997) *The Inner Game of Work*. Villard Books

Gerber, M. (2001) *The E-Myth Revisited: Why most small businesses don't work and what to do about it*. HarperBusiness

Goleman, D. (1996) *Emotional Intelligence: Why it can matter more than IQ*. Bloomsbury

Goldsmith, M. (2008) *What Got You Here Won't Get You There: How successful people become even more successful*. Profile Books

Hudson, F. and McLean, P. (2011) *LifeLaunch: A passionate guide to the rest of your life* 5th edition. The Hudson Institute Press

Kline, N. (2002) *Time to Think: Listening to ignite the human mind*. Cassell

Kramer, G. (2012) *Stillpower: Excellence with ease in sports and life*. Greenleaf Book Group LLC

Laborde, G. (1995) *Influencing With Integrity: Management skills for communication and negotiation*. Crown House Publishing

Maister, D., Green, C. and Galford, R. (2002) *The Trusted Advisor*. Simon and Schulster UK Ltd

Neill, M. (2013) *The Inside-out Revolution: The only thing you need to know to change your life forever*. Hay House UK

Pine II, J. and Gilmore, J. (2011) *The Experience Economy, Updated Edition*. Harvard Business School Press

Pransky, G. (2013) *The Relationship Handbook*. Pransky and Associates

Raia, M. (2014) Make them an offer they can't refuse. 4 February 2014. TranStrategy Partners: blog. <http://www.transtrategypartners.com/blogdetail.php?id=96>

Spittle, E. (2010) *Our True Identity ...Three Principles*. CreateSpace Independent Publishing Platform

About John Dashfield

John is a transformational coach, mentor and writer specialising in the financial services sector. He brings a new, fresh and unique approach to helping advisers and firms to be truly 'client centred' and create a thriving, sustainable practice.

John's financial services journey began in 1986 when he took a job at the head office of an international life company. His role was as a pension's technical adviser to the company's financial advisers. After regularly speaking with many of the advisers he was inspired to join them and became a self-employed financial adviser in 1991. After a few years he set up his own independent practice.

In 2002 he began to follow his interest in coaching people and sold his financial practice in 2005 to concentrate solely on coaching and mentoring. Since then he has worked with individuals and firms all over the UK as well as clients in Europe, Australia and the US.

John lives with his family in rural Kent.

What we do

John offers a unique approach for practitioners and practices committed to becoming 'client centred' and performing at their best ever levels.

The foundation for all of our coaching and mentoring programmes is sharing an understanding of state of mind and what creates it. Refreshingly, there are no techniques, methods or practices to undertake and yet this foundation gives you everything you need to make quantum leaps in your performance and results. Typically, our clients experience significant improvements in:

- Their ability to build trust, rapport and connection
- How well and how deeply they engage their clients
- How clearly they see opportunity and respond to it
- Their levels of resilience
- Their decision-making ability
- Their ability to lead others
- How well and quickly they solve problems
- Their levels of overall performance
- Their sense of personal wellbeing
- The reduction and elimination of stress

To join our community please visit www.clientcentredadvisers.com where you can subscribe to our blog, find further resources and discover 'The top 10 client conversation mistakes'.

You can contact John Dashfield:

Email: john@clientcentredadvisers.com

Telephone: +44(0)7860 682530